The ⸱
ASHUA

A S H I S H   S A H

BlueRose ONE
Stories Matter
NewDelhi • London

BLUEROSE PUBLISHERS
India | U.K.

For permissions requests or inquiries regarding this publication, please contact:

BLUEROSE PUBLISHERS
www.BlueRoseONE.com
info@bluerosepublishers.com
+91 8882 898 898
+4407342408967

ISBN: 978-93-5819-700-6

Cover design: Tahira
Typesetting: Tanya Raj Upadhyay

First Edition: December 2023

THE TALE
OF
ASHUA

Ddedicated to to my father Late Mr. Harish Chandra Sah and my faimly from Chaubattia

Chapter 1

nce upon a time, knowledge was a scarce commodity, reserved for a select few. But in today's interconnected world, information flows freely and abundantly, reaching the farthest corners. Today, I invite you to uncover the intriguing story of an enigmatic figure named Ashua. Not everyone possesses the ability to rise from the ashes, but some who do become the stuff of legends. Ashua was one such person, and it is my privilege to share his extraordinary tale with you.

Ashua resided in the tiny village of Magaon, nestled at the foothills of the majestic Himalayas. Magaon was surrounded by dense oak forests, teeming with a wide array of wild animals. Leopards and tigers roamed freely in the woods, occasionally preying on the village's domesticated animals, like goats. With a deep familiarity of the forest, Ashua knew its paths and secrets like the back of his hand. For 18 years, he had shepherded his goats amidst those ancient trees. Yet, deep within his heart, Ashua longed for something substantial, a desire to make his father, affectionately known as Babuji, proud.

Magaon was a close-knit community, comprised of twenty or thirty families dwelling in small wooden houses, huddled together. Every villager emanated warmth and vitality, creating an atmosphere of unity and care. Each person knew each other. They were like one big family, mutually dependent on each other.

However, Magaon faced a significant challenge. With limited options available, the villagers primarily relied on cattle raising and seasonal crop cultivation to make ends meet. Barley thrived during the winter, while wheat flourished in the summer. Although vegetables were cultivated year-round, the harvest merely met their daily needs, leaving no surplus for trade or sale.

It was no wonder that the young souls of Magaon yearned to escape the village's confines and seek a better life in the city. The urban world enticed them with promises of prosperity and excitement, a world they idealized without understanding its complexities. As the saying goes, the grass is always greener on the other side.

Ashua, a young mountain boy with a modest stature, possessed eyes that shimmered with an undeniable radiance. His eyes were small but they had something in them that made him stand out of the realm. His ever-present smile charmed all who encountered him, even during the most challenging times.

Each frigid winter morning, just before the break of dawn, Ashua would rise from his bed, prepare tea for his father, and make his way to the barn to attend to his goats. As he slowly swung open the barn doors, revealing his flock of twenty-one goats nestled together, a wave of relief washed over him.

Another day dawned, marking the beginning of Ashua's journey.

He possessed an innate discipline, a quality he had never consciously acknowledged or contemplated before. Little did he know that this unwavering discipline would propel him on a remarkable path through the twists and turns of life. Regardless of the weather, whether the air was frigid or scorching hot, Ashua never lingered in bed beyond dawn. This unwavering commitment permeated every aspect of his existence. Laziness was a foreign concept to him, as he was consumed by the multitude of responsibilities that demanded his attention. Life in the hills was unforgiving. Navigating from one place to another necessitated scaling steep mountains, only to descend on the other side.

As the sun cast its radiant embrace upon the land, awakening the surroundings, the village came alive bustling with activity. Mukesh, the milkman, diligently milked his cows, while Radha and the other village women ventured into the fields to sow the seeds for the forthcoming harvest. The rhythmic clang of Ramji's hammer resonated through the village, as he fashioned iron into useful creations.

Life in the village was a formidable existence, an enigma beyond the comprehension of city dwellers. For the people of Magaon, it was a ceaseless cycle of toil. "Work, work, all day long" was their anthem. Every day mirrored the previous one, with no intervals or Sundays to break the monotony. Holidays were an unattainable luxury, a concept foreign to their reality.

Life, at times, seemed unjust and unfair. Some toiled tirelessly in the fields, their hands dirtied and sweat-soaked, earning a mere pittance. Meanwhile, others effortlessly amassed wealth, reaping the rewards of minimal exertion. Such was the dichotomy of existence.

While the villagers of Magaon were content with their modest ambitions and desires, Ashua stood apart from the rest. He possessed a unique perspective on life and nurtured aspirations that extended beyond the boundaries of his small village. Eager to carve a meaningful existence for himself, Ashua patiently waited for the right opportunity to grace him. He held an unwavering belief that an opportunity would manifest itself, though he was not sure when. Blessed with the patience of a saint, he embraced the tranquility that accompanies waiting, knowing that when the time was right, his path would be illuminated.

Ashua meticulously counted his growing herd of fat and robust goats, a testament to his unwavering dedication and care. With a tender smile, he informed his father, "Babuji, I am heading to the mountains to feed the goats."

In response, Babuji, Ashua's beloved father whose real name was Harda, affectionately replied, "Alright, Ashua. Take good care of yourself. May God watch over you."

Babuji's aging appearance, marked by the etchings of time on his face, deeply concerned Ashua. Witnessing his father's frailty and vulnerability weighed heavily on his heart. Moreover, Babuji's health issues, including frequent bouts of illness and ailing heart, added to the burden. However, the absence of doctors in the village meant that the true extent of Babuji's ailments remained unknown.

Harda was a diligent peasant who had devoted his entire life to working in Magaon and raising his two sons, Ashua and Ramesh. Despite limited resources, Harda managed to provide his sons with a basic education, equipping them with the skills necessary to navigate the literate world. Ramesh, the elder son, had ventured to the city, where he married the love of his life and found employment in a restaurant. Though Ramesh seemed less concerned about the family, Babuji, like any proud father, still held him in high regard.

Meanwhile, Ashua constantly sought greener pastures for his goats. He strived to find the best grasslands for his four-legged companions, ensuring they grew strong and healthy. His goal was to sell them at a favorable price, earning him some much-needed income.

He was looking for greener pastures in his life also, waiting for the right opportunity to come his way He approached every task with his utmost dedication, regardless of its scale or significance; he believed that effort was crucial in achieving success. You have to give your best in whatever you do.

As he ascended the hill, following the winding path overshadowed by towering fern trees, Ashua's thoughts wandered to his brother, Ramesh, who had ventured to the city of Charbattia. Ramesh had left for Charbattia several years ago and had since settled there. He would occasionally send them money as he had a job in the city but it had been a long time and no money had come from his end. Ramesh hardly came to Magaon and Ashua missed him deeply. Ashua wanted to ask Ramesh for something that he wanted desperately. It was something as important as air to him. But Ramesh was far away in the city and all efforts to connect to him were futile.

Ashua trudged along the path that led him to the top of the hill. As he reached the end of the narrow path, a breathtaking meadow unfolded before his eyes, resplendent in shades of green. A gentle stream, adorned with crystal-clear water, cascaded down the hillside. A wave of relief washed over Ashua as he arrived at his destination at just the right time. Now his tender pets could nibble the whole day. He approached the stream and joyfully splashed the cold, refreshing water on his face, rejuvenating himself. As far as his eyes could see, there were no people in sight, only the vast expanse of the blue sky adorned with fluffy white clouds.

Ashua was not a well-read person. Although he had attended the village school for his primary education, he yearned for further studies. However, financial constraints forced him to drop out after completing high school. The education he received provided him with the basics to navigate the fiercely competitive world. But that was enough for Ashua to chase his dreams although he desired to study further.

In Magaon, completing high school was a rare achievement, but Ashua's determination and hard work allowed him to accomplish this feat on his first attempt. This success filled him with a sense of pride and accomplishment.

On the top of the mountain as the cool breeze gently touched Ashua's face it suddenly occurred to him that people were talking of some light being seen on the hill. There were rounds in the village and people were gossiping that a mysterious yellow light was seen up on the hill for the past few days. And no one knew what it was. Ashua was curious just like everyone to know what that light was so he decided to explore the place. Ashua walked along the ridge of the hill, taking in the breathtaking scenery that unfolded before his eyes. It was as if an artist had painted something on a big canvas before him. From this vantage point, he could see the lush green fields of his village stretching out below. It was as if he had been granted a bird's-eye view of his beloved village. The sight was nothing short of awe-inspiring. The vibrant colors of the fields and the quaint little houses resembled a beautiful, serene painting carefully crafted by a talented artist.

As Ashua continued walking along the ridge, he noticed an old dilapidated temple in the distance. The sight of it was unexpected in this remote part of the jungle up on the hill. There was some kind of eeriness attached to the place. The air around the temple was heavy with silence, and Ashua could feel his heart pounding in his chest. The whole place was unusually calm and still.

Legend had it that the temple carried a curse, with whispers spreading through the village about anyone who entered meeting a tragic fate. But Ashua chose to disregard these stories and approached the temple with determination.It seemed that no one had visited the temple in ages. As the distance between Ashua and the temple got narrower and narrower fear began to grip Ashua. But Ashua mustered all the courage he could and kept walking towards the temple.

As Ashua approached the temple, its ancient stone structure became more visible, surrounded by towering fern trees. The temple stood on a flat piece of land amidst the hills, engulfed by the encroaching forest. The green moss that covered its surfaces added to its eerie aura, as if nature itself had claimed the temple as its own.

Curiosity filled Ashua's mind as he meticulously examined the surroundings, paying attention to every detail. Then, something caught his eye and left him astonished. It appeared that someone had visited the temple recently, as the grass just outside the temple had been tempered. But who would venture to this desolate place that had long been forgotten by the outside world?

Suddenly, a noise reached Ashua's ears from behind the temple, jolting him with alarm. Was it a thud or simply his imagination running wild? The sound of footsteps grew clearer, indicating that someone was sneaking around behind the temple. Ashua's fear froze him in place. Who could be present at such an unusual hour in such a secluded location?

As adrenaline began pumping through his veins, Ashua's first instinct was to flee down the hill toward his village and be gone. However, he took a moment to gather himself, inhaling a deep breath of cold air into his lungs. After careful consideration, he resolved that it was best to investigate and find out who or what was lurking behind the temple. Summoning all his courage, Ashua moved cautiously behind the temple, determined to uncover the mystery that awaited him.

Fueled by concern for his goats' safety and the potential threat of wild animals or bandits, Ashua cautiously ventured behind the temple to uncover the source of the footsteps. The sound grew louder and more rapid, suggesting the creature was hastening its pace. Determined, Ashua chased after it, relying on the sound of the reverberating footsteps as his guide. His speed intensified as he relentlessly pursued the mysterious entity, eagerly anticipating the moment he would lay eyes upon it.

Suddenly, his pursuit came to a halt, leaving Ashua dumbfounded. What stood before him was neither an animal nor a bandit—it was an old man dressed in an orange robe, effortlessly gliding through the air. The sight of the elderly monk left Ashua stunned and unsure of how to react. The monk appeared too elderly to run, yet here he was, defying gravity with his ethereal movement. Overwhelmed by disbelief, Ashua found himself at a loss for words and actions.

Summoning every ounce of courage he possessed, Ashua managed to gather enough air in his lungs to shout, "STOP! STOP!" The exertion from his sprint made it difficult to speak, but he hoped his plea would reach the enigmatic monk. To his surprise, the monk momentarily halted his graceful glide and turned his gaze directly toward Ashua, their eyes meeting in an intense moment of connection.

Ashua remained in awe as he beheld the yogi before him. The monk's presence radiated an otherworldly aura, with a face untouched by wrinkles and a physique that defied his apparent age. His white beard cascaded gracefully, and his flowing locks mirrored the serenity that enveloped him. Clad in his flowing orange robe, the yogi seemed to embody wisdom and spiritual vitality. The yogis of the Himalayas were said to possess extraordinary longevity, rumored to have lived through centuries.

Having grown up listening to tales of these mystical beings in folk tales and legends, Ashua considered himself blessed to witness the presence of a Himalayan yogi. It was an uncommon and almost surreal occurrence to have direct sight of one. According to the stories, receiving the blessings of a Himalayan yogi could bring about the materialization of one's desires and the resolution of all problems. Overwhelmed with reverence and a deep sense of longing, Ashua instinctively kneeled before the yogi, closing his eyes in prayer.

In a hushed tone, Ashua whispered, "O Holy One, please bless me and grant the fulfillment of my desires and wishes." His entire being was immersed in his prayer, as if transported into a trance-like state focused solely on the yogi. Within the depths of his consciousness, he sought a connection with the divine soul standing before him.

Suddenly, a voice resonated in Ashua's mind, distinct and yet ethereal. "Get up, young man." Ashua obediently opened his eyes, only to be met with a tender smile from the yogi. There was an inexplicable allure in the yogi's presence that compelled one to remain captivated and gaze upon him. It felt as if a divine communion was taking place, with the yogi attempting to communicate telepathically.

A voice echoed in Ashua's head once more, assuring him, "You are a good soul, young man. Your essence remains pure." These words humbled Ashua, though their true meaning eluded him. He sensed that the divine soul intended to convey a profound message, yet he remained unsure of its full significance.

Once again, the voice reverberated in Ashua's mind, imparting its wisdom. "Not all can see or hear me, young man. Only those with a golden heart and pure intentions possess the ability to perceive my presence. In a world widespread with falsehoods, deceit, and treachery, you stand as a rare entity and genuine soul."

Curiosity burning within him, Ashua mustered the courage to ask, "Who are you, and from where do you come, O great one?"

The voice responded, "I am a wanderer, devoid of a fixed abode. I move as my spirit guides me, transcending the constraints of time. But you, young man, have a purpose to fulfill within the limited time bestowed upon you by the divine. Time, the most precious of commodities, holds greater value than mere wealth. While money lost can be regained, time lost can never be reclaimed. Just as you wisely manage your finances, consider investing your time with equal care."

Ashua's voice took on a somber tone as he replied, "I am but a humble village boy with limited means and opportunities. There is little I can do to change my circumstances. Please, guide me, O great one."

Once again, the voice resounded in Ashua's consciousness, driving home its message. "In the eyes of the Divine, no one is deemed small or insignificant. God grants equal opportunities to all, and it is the individual's choice whether to seize them or let them pass it on to someone else. Some individuals grasp these opportunities, utilizing them as stepping stones to realize their dreams and aspirations. Others, however, relinquish them. Therefore, when an opportunity presents itself, do not let it pass you by."

The message struck Ashua's heart with clarity, like the expansive blue sky above him. Wisdom bathed his being, and the yogi's words revealed that his journey was far from over. No one held the power to alter the trajectory of Ashua's life but he himself. It was simply a matter of time and patience.

Ashua's spirit was reignited, and he realized that having big dreams and aspirations was not a futile pursuit. Those people who mock other people's dreams are belittled dreamers who lack the courage to pursue their own dreams. He understood that dreams could only transform into achievable goals when accompanied by unwavering dedication and hard work – something Ashua was not afraid of. He embraced the challenges and was ready to invest his best efforts into any venture he took on. However, he also recognized that perhaps it was not his time just yet. He had to wait.

Doubts began to seep into Ashua's mind as he contemplated the hurdles that lay ahead. How could he ever achieve his dream of becoming a vertical in the society and gaining the love and respect of the society? His limited education and financial constraints seemed insurmountable barriers, even if an opportunity did present itself. The feeling of life's unfairness and helplessness weighed heavily on him, leaving him disheartened.

But the wise words of the yogi echoed once more, breaking through Ashua's despondency. "Remember, young man, nothing is impossible. Though challenges may seem daunting and quitting may appear like the best thing, but giving up is never a solution. When you find yourself in rough waters, will you let yourself drown? No! Seek solution, for every problem there has to be a solution. As there is an antidote for every venom, same way there is a solution to every problem. If you seek success, respect, and wealth, you will achieve them, but it demands relentless effort and determination."

The yogi's guidance served as a beacon of hope for Ashua, illuminating his path forward. He understood that every obstacle was an opportunity in disguise, waiting for him to unravel it. Instead of dwelling on his present circumstances, he vowed to be proactive and resilient in the face of adversity. With renewed vigor,

Ashua decided to embrace the journey ahead, for he knew that with unyielding dedication, his dreams would eventually become reality.

Tears of joy began streaming down his face, as now Ashua had a purpose in life. Ashua gazed at the spot where the yogi had stood, his hands still folded in reverence. He implored, "O Great One, continue to bless and guide me on my journey through life. When I lose my way and deviate from the path of righteousness, please steer me back, and I hope to never disappoint you."

The yogi, with a serene smile, responded, "Listen, young man, keep your faith unwavering in the almighty. He desires the best for all. Hope and faith are the two most powerful weapons at your disposal to fight against adversity. Believe in yourself and in the divine, for there is nothing you cannot achieve. Keep the flame of hope burning within you at all times. As long as you hold onto hope, no one can hinder your progress."

With these parting words, the yogi turned toward the forest and, as swiftly as he had arrived, vanished from sight. Ashua was left in awe, unsure if what had transpired was a dream or a tangible encounter. It felt as if time itself had frozen during their conversation.

Hastily, he approached the spot where the yogi had stood moments ago and gently touched the ground. The earth bore the imprint of the yogi's presence, solidifying the reality of his life-changing encounter. Overwhelmed, Ashua sat there in disbelief, closed his eyes, and wept. He had been revitalized, and most importantly, he had been bestowed with a purpose—a purpose that was yet to be fully revealed.

Regaining his composure, Ashua looked up at the darkening sky. The sun was nearing its descent, signaling the approaching nightfall. Hours had slipped away since he had arrived at the hilltop, yet to Ashua, it felt as if only minutes had passed. He realized he needed to hurry back to the village before darkness engulfed the surroundings, for the forest would soon be teeming with wild animals. Moreover, his absence would surely have Babuji, his father, deeply worried. With a renewed sense of urgency, Ashua rushed towards his goats, who were leisurely grazing on the lush green grass, and gently guided them down the hill.

As Ashua was walking down the hill he was observing the simplicity of the animals' lives. Animals were free spirits, unburdened by the complexities of thought and purpose. They thrived on fulfilling their basic needs, reproducing, and eventually becoming a source of nourishment for a lucky family. Their lives were uncomplicated, whereas humans had woven intricate webs of complications that deprived them of peace. Their minds raced faster than light, perpetually fixated on an uncertain and elusive future. It had been rightly said, "The past brings forth depression, and the future breeds anxiety, so it is best to dwell in the present."

With these reflections in his heart, Ashua continued his descent, determined to navigate the challenges that lay ahead and embrace the purpose that awaited him.

Ashua quickly counted his goats and began to hurry down the mountain toward his village. Along the way, as he was busy guiding his goats down the right track to his village, he was thinking about the remarkable turn of events that had happened today. He was captivated by the yogi. An event had taken place that had changed his life and got back his confidence that he was gradually fading with time.

As he trudged along the twisted narrow path down the hill, he heard a howl. Now wolves were nearby, so he had to hurry. The dusk had set in, and the sky was painted with a red-orange hue, which looked beautiful. But it was not a time to admire nature's beauty, but to rush home as the howling of the wolves was getting clearer and nearer. After a brisk walk down the hill, Ashua reached the village, and he was thankful that he had reached his home safe and sound.

Ashua locked his goats in the tiny shabby barn, which was just outside the house where they lived, and entered his house. The house where they lived was always warm and cozy. It was a wooden structure just like any other house in the village, and Babuji had himself built it a long time ago. A house is warm and cozy as long as people inside the house are loving and caring. If people hate and despise each other, then the same house becomes cold, and harshness will choke you to death. But Ashua and his father loved each other, and they were like pillars of strength for each other. The bond between Ashua and Babuji could not be described in words. They could lay their lives for each other when the time came, but not today, as Ashua could smell that dinner was being cooked and the fire stove was burning to fight the bitter cold and give them warmth.

As soon as Ashua entered his house, things were not the same as before. Babuji, who would wait for

Ashua every day when he returned, with a hot cup of tea and something to eat, was not there. He was talking to someone in the kitchen, and muffled sounds could be heard. As Ashua made his way to the kitchen, he was greeted by a pleasant surprise. Guess who was there? It was his brother, Ramesh. This was completely unexpected. Ashua was filled with joy and excitement. He rushed towards Ramesh and embraced him tightly, tears streaming down his cheeks. Ramesh was a little surprised by this reaction, but he hugged Ashua back. Babuji stood there, smiling proudly, knowing that he had been successfully in raising his sons after the tragic loss of their mother, whom he loved dearly. The immense love and respect the brothers had for each other was an extraordinary sight.

Ashua asked Ramesh with excitement, "When did you arrive here, brother?"

Ramesh replied plainly, "I arrived when you had gone to the mountains to feed the goats. How is everything?"

"All good," Ashua said.

"Ramesh, it's been a long time since you came to Magaon. Is city life so good that you forgot us?" Ashua teased.

"It's a very busy life in the city, Ashua. I hope you can understand. There are lot of other things that are to be taken care of" Ramesh replied, sounding slightly annoyed.

Babuji interrupted the boys, saying, "So, are you both going to keep talking or are we going to have the dinner I just cooked?"

The two brothers sat down on the ground, just like in the old days, and started eating the dinner Babuji had prepared. The aroma of the meal was smoky, as it was cooked on a wooden stove. It felt like the good old times. While enjoying their meal, Ashua grew increasingly uneasy. There was a question he had been longing to ask Ramesh, but he didn't want to spoil the moment, so he kept it to himself. He knew he had to wait for the right time. Patience is a virtue, and the impact is enhanced when the right words are spoken at the right moment. So, he had to wait a little longer.

After dinner, the brothers had a glass of milk, as it was a village routine before bedtime. Ramesh, exhausted from the long journey, fell fast asleep. However, Ashua couldn't find sleep that night. He always carried a burning desire in his heart to go to the city. In the city, his dreams could be realized. The city held the key to becoming a wealthy and successful person, someone Babuji would be proud of. In the village, no matter how hard he worked, he could barely make ends meet. Survival was a struggle, whereas in the city, numerous opportunities awaited him. The city was full of endless possibilities, while the village offered scarce opportunities and limited earnings. Ashua didn't want to remain trapped in the village for the rest of his life. He yearned for a better life not only for himself but also for Babuji. If things went according to plan, he even wanted to contribute something to the village, perhaps by building a hospital.

The night passed slowly for Ashua, while Ramesh snored peacefully.

Early the next morning, Ashua woke up and as he walked outside he overheard Ramesh and Babuji discussing something important.

Ashua had conceived a notion to share his plans of leaving the village and going to the city with Ramesh. His strategy was simple: he would stay with Ramesh for a while, find a job, and then send money back home to Babuji. Once settled, he would search for a place to stay in the city. He knew there would be disagreement, as

Babuji relied on him as the only support in the village, but he was prepared for an argument.

As Ashua mustered up the courage to approach his father with a heavy heart, Ramesh, who was with Babuji, suddenly called out to Ashua and sternly said, "We want to talk to you about something important, Ashua. Come and join us."

Ashua became anxious, wondering if his brother knew about his plan, but he had never discussed it with him before. Ashua was rattled as he looked into Ramesh's eyes and asked, "What do you want to speak to me about?"

In a soft tone, Ramesh tried to convey the message to Ashua in the best possible manner, saying, "Babuji and I were discussing that you are now old enough to take care of yourself. It is time for you to settle down and get married."

Ashua didn't see this coming; he was taken aback. He felt furious as this was not what he had expected.

Babuji added, "Ashua, my son, you must find a girl and get married."

"But, Babuji..." Ashua began.

Interrupting him, Babuji continued, "Everyone has to get married. I won't be here forever, and someone needs to be with you to take care of you, my son. When you were born, I vowed to take care of you. Now that you're a grown man, it is time for you to get married and raise a family."

Ashua's rage grew, and he angrily responded, "No, Babuji, I don't want to get married."

Babuji persisted, "You must find a partner who will be your friend, companion, and soul mate. Marriage is a sacred institution, and you must commit to it. My life wouldn't have been the same without your mother. I still think of her, even though she's no longer with us. She gave me a reason to live; she gave me both of you. So, please reconsider your decision and get married." Tears welled up in Babuji's eyes.

Ashua retorted, "Listen, Babuji, it's not that I don't want to get married, but I have other plans right now. I have a whole life ahead of me, and someday, I will get married. But right now, I want to go to the city, work, and make some money so that we all can lead a better life."

Ramesh chimed in, "Working in the city isn't easy; not everyone can survive there. Don't be ridiculous."

To which Ashua replied firmly, "It's not easy here either. I deserve a chance to go to the city, and if I don't succeed, I will come back to Magaon. But I must go with you."

As the discussion grew heated between the brothers, Babuji rose from his chair, took a deep breath, and passed his judgment, saying, "Ashua, life is full of challenges, and if you take up a challenge, you must see it through. You will go to the city of Charbattia with Ramesh, but you must not come back as a loser."

The verdict had been delivered, and both parties had to abide by it. Babuji recognized Ashua's potential and understood him better than Ashua might have known himself. The decision was made because Babuji knew Ashua was not a quitter. Babuji knew that when Ashua sets his mind to do something, he would overcome any obstacles in his path to attain it. Ashua possessed talents and gifts beyond what Ramesh was capable of, that is why Babuji nodded in agreement to Ashua's decision to pursue his dreams in Charbattia.

The next day, Ramesh and Ashua were ready to set off to Charbattia. Before they left, Babuji called Ashua close and whispered in his ear, "Listen, my son. You're going to a place you've never been before. I've heard that people there can be deceptive. Don't trust anyone easily; use your wits in all situations. Ramesh will take care of you, but don't become a burden on him. No one wants an unnecessary burden. Here, take some money. It's not much, but keep it."

Ashua hesitated and said, "No, Babuji, I cannot take this money."

Babuji insisted, "Take it. This money will come in handy when you face difficult times. Use it wisely."

With tears in their eyes, Babuji and Ashua embraced each other for one last time. As Ashua and Ramesh boarded the local bus that would take them to the nearby railway station, Babuji stood there, waiting and waving his hands, unaware of when his two precious gems would return to Magaon. He felt a sense of sadness and heartbreak, but he knew he was not the only father in the village experiencing such emotions. He had to find courage to endure the pain. The last thing he wanted had happened; Ashua had left him for the city.

Thus, a new journey was about to begin for Ashua, who had spent all his life tending to goats in Magaon. With unwavering determination, he embarked on the path to Charbattia alongside his elder brother, unaware of what lay ahead.

Summary

Dreaming is not a waste of time.

Chapter 2

Ashua and Ramesh arrived in Charbattia - the City of Dreams. As soon as Ashua stepped out of the train compartment and set foot on the soil of Charbattia, he instantly felt out of his comfort zone. The scorching sun beat down on him, causing him to sweat profusely, and the polluted city air made it difficult for him to breathe.

The railway station in Charbattia was a scene of utter chaos. It was filled with a multitude of random people. In Magaon, his small village, things were different. You knew everyone living there and there was a sense of connection among the residents. They relied on each other for survival and interacted regularly with each other. Here, in Charbattia, it was a mad rush. People were everywhere, unconnected and unfamiliar. It would take a lifetime to get to know them all.

Yet, amidst the chaos, there was a certain beauty attached to the place. The railway station was vibrant and filled with colors. People from all walks of life, dressed in various bright attires, could be seen everywhere. Rich and poor, people of all backgrounds walked together. For Ashua, it wasn't just a city; it was like a whole new country.

This city was kind to those who dared to chase their dreams, undeterred by their adversities and problems. However, for most people, the city was harsh. Charbattia was known as the graveyard of broken dreams, claiming the lives of countless dreamers who had come with great hope to make it big in the city. But strangely, most people never returned to their native towns after coming to the city. They stayed, making compromise after compromise with themselves and their dreams until their dreams were finally extinguished. So, one must not be fooled by the tall buildings and luxury cars that lined the streets.

After retrieving their luggage from the railway station, they boarded a local bus that would take them to Ramesh's place. Ashua secured a window seat, and as the bus maneuvered through the congested roads, he stuck his head out and was overwhelmed by the sights. Tall buildings and advertisement billboards adorned the sides of the road. Cars and trucks crowded the streets, while vendors sold a variety of items, from clothing to electronics, on the roadside. Everyone seemed to be in a hurry. Ashua was amazed, having been accustomed to seeing tall fern trees in his village, but now those visuals had been replaced by these towering skyscrapers. The lush greenery of his village had given way to concrete structures. No one in the village owned a car, but here it seemed like everyone had one. Excitement and nervousness surged within him simultaneously. But he was very excited being there in Charbattia.

After an hour-long ride, the bus came to a halt.

Ramesh weakly told Ashua, "We have reached our destination."

Ashua sensed that something was bothering Ramesh as Ramesh was sweating profoundly.

The two brothers stepped off the bus. Ashua was overflowing with excitement, like a child in a new playground. However, Ramesh was filled with worry, uncertain of how his wife Meena would react upon seeing Ashua.

Ramesh and Meena had been married for two years, but they had little in common. Ramesh was content with the simple life he had in the village, while Meena, born and raised in the city, was always dissatisfied with their modest lifestyle. She often felt trapped in her marriage with Ramesh, and they were far from being an ideal match.

As Ramesh and Ashua climbed the stairs to their apartment on the second floor of a dilapidated building, Ashua's emotions became mixed. Ramesh knocked on the door, and Meena hastily opened it.

As the brothers entered the apartment, Meena greeted them with a smile. She cheerfully asked, "How was the journey?"

Ramesh replied, "It was good," and continued, "I have a surprise for you," introducing Ashua to Meena. Ashua was thrilled to see Meena again. Eagerly, he said, "How are you, Meena?"

Meena looked at Ashua and replied, "I am good," before returning to the kitchen.

Having lost his mother at a young age and lacking female figures in the family, Ashua considered Meena to be a motherly figure. Although he had only met her a few times when she visited their village, he held great respect for her. However, today felt different.

Ashua was closely observing Meena from a distance.

He saw Meena looked uneasy. Hesensed that she was not pleased with his arrival. He felt a bit awkward as if he was like a stranger in his brother's house. However, he hoped that with time, the ice between them would melt.

In the evening, Ashua and Ramesh sat down for dinner, which Meena had prepared. Meena, a tall and slim woman with a dusky complexion, had been visibly upset since Ramesh's return from Magaon. Ramesh had a vague idea of what was troubling her. Meena placed the food on the table, and Ashua, who was famished from not having eaten since leaving his village, eagerly devoured the rice and dal that Meena had cooked.

While Ashua was engrossed in his meal, Ramesh interrupted him and said, "Tomorrow, I will take you to the restaurant where I work and talk to Mr. Seth. Maybe he has a job for you. Mr. Seth is a kind man, and I have been working for him for some time now. He could be of help to us."

After dinner, Ramesh gave Ashua a blanket and instructed him to sleep in one of the rooms, preparing for tomorrow's meeting, which Ashua was eagerly looking forward to. Ramesh went inside to sleep in his room with Meena, who was anxiously awaiting his arrival.

After entering the room, Ramesh found Meena waiting for him, seething with anger. She shouted, "Are our troubles not enough that you have brought that boy along to add to our miseries? You should have consulted me before bringing him here!"

Ramesh, in a feeble voice, muttered, "It happened so quickly, I couldn't do anything."

Meena's rage intensified, and she warned Ramesh, "He eats like a pig. I am not going to cook for him."

Weakly, Ramesh pleaded, "Please, stop this. He is my only brother, and I promised Babuji that I will take care of him."

Meena, with firmness in her voice, issued an ultimatum, saying, "Either I stay, or you throw that person out of the house. The choice is yours."

The room fell into a silence that felt lifeless and ominous. In the adjacent room, Ashua eavesdropped on the entire conversation, lying on his bed, frozen with terror. Tears welled up in his eyes, and fear engulfed him. He trembled with the thought of his brother casting him out. Where would he go then?

Throughout the night, Ashua was unable to sleep, consumed by worry, while Meena eventually drifted off, unaware of the turmoil she had unleashed upon the family.

As the next morning dawned, the city was shrouded in a gloomy and overcast atmosphere. A thick layer of clouds hung in the sky, and a dense fog had blanketed the entire city, casting a spell of uncertainty and apprehension.

Ashua woke up early as usual, dressed in his finest attire, and eagerly awaited Ramesh to take him to meet Mr. Seth. Ramesh, appearing sad and worried, remained silent, leaving Ashua uncertain about his fate. However, as Ramesh said nothing, Ashua found reassurance that perhaps the previous night's conversation was a product of his imagination or overthinking due to fatigue from the journey. His happiness was restored, and he maintained hope that nothing dreadful would occur.

The brothers boarded a bus that dropped them off at the renowned restaurant, "DARBAR." Among the many branches in Charbattia, this particular location stood out as the crown jewel, known for its elegance and superior dining experience. Although Ramesh didn't work at this branch, Mr. Seth, the head of operations for "DARBAR," had his office there.

Stepping into the restaurant, Ashua was astounded by its grandeur. The spacious dining area could accommodate a hundred people, with neatly arranged tables and chairs adorned with white tablecloths. The pendant lighting hanging from the ceiling added an elegant touch, unlike anything Ashua had ever seen. Deep down, he had a strong desire to work in such a fancy establishment.

As Ramesh led him toward Mr. Seth's office, Ashua's anxiety grew. They cautiously entered the cabin, and there sat Mr. Seth—a middle-aged man with a protruding belly and a bald head. It was evident he had been in the business for quite some time, as his hawk-like eyes scanned Ramesh and asked, "What brings you here, Ramesh?"

Ramesh introduced Ashua, saying, "Sir, this is Ashua, my brother, and he wishes to work here at the restaurant."

In a firm tone, Mr. Seth responded, "We don't hire people in such an impromptu manner. We have a standard procedure that must be followed, and you are well aware of it."

Ashua felt a surge of electricity pass through his body, momentarily unsettling him. However, Ramesh, in a frantic tone, made a heartfelt plea, "But Sir, he is my younger brother. He has left his village and has come a long way to work here. I hope you understand."

Mr. Seth initially seemed inclined to reject the request, but as he observed Ashua closely, he saw something remarkable in his eyes—innocence coupled with immense desperation. Those small, brown eyes conveyed a story of a young man in need of a job, willing to go to any lengths to secure one. Mr. Seth also recognized Ashua's unwavering determination and discipline that would make him an exemplary employee. It was evident that Ashua would not disappoint. With limited options and nowhere else to go, he possessed the attributes that every employer sought.

Fixing his gaze on Ashua, Mr. Seth sternly inquired, "Why should I hire you, young man? Have you worked in any other restaurant before?"

With unwavering confidence, Ashua responded, "Sir, while I haven't worked in any restaurant previously, I assure you that I have never shied away from hard work. I am a quick learner and a better retainer. I never forget what I have been taught, and I do not give up easily. No task is too small or menial for me. I will work diligently, with honesty and integrity, giving my best in everything I do. You can count on me."

This resolute answer to a common job interview question impressed Mr. Seth. He was struck by Ashua's level of honesty and decided to hire him on the spot. Mr. Seth stated, "Alright, Ashua, you will receive a fixed monthly salary of Rs 10,000 and I will send someone who will tell you what your duties are here at the restaurant."

After bidding farewell to Mr. Seth, Ashua felt tears of joy streaming down his face. It was as if he had won a lottery ticket, a ticket to stay in Charbattia. Ramesh embraced him tightly before hurriedly leaving for work.

As Ashua collected himself, a young man named Vikas entered the room to meet him. Vikas looked like an educated young man but looks are often deceiving. Vikas, a few years older than Ashua, also worked at "DARBAR" as a waiter, diligently serving hot meals to the hungry customers. Vikas wore a warm smile as he welcomed Ashua into their fraternity.

"Let me guess, you must be Ashua. Congratulations! I heard you're the new arrival in the restaurant," Vikas greeted him. "Mr. Seth just informed me to show you around the place where you'll be working."

Instantly engaging in conversation, Ashua bombarded Vikas with a series of questions. "Where do you stay, Vikas? Are you from Charbattia? And what exactly do you do here at the restaurant?"

Vikas eagerly responded to Ashua's inquiries. "I stay in a humble apartment near the restaurant, Ashua. I came to Charbattia four years ago in search of employment and have been working here ever since. My role involves taking orders from customers and serving them steaming hot meals, prepared by Mr. Lalit, our head chef at DARBAR."

Following their brief conversation, Vikas proceeded to give Ashua a tour of the restaurant. He showed him the designated area where Ashua would be working and explained, "This is the kitchen where you'll be stationed. Once the customers finish their meals, the dirty plates will come here, and it will be your responsibility to wash them thoroughly and ensure they're impeccably clean."

Vikas handed Ashua the staff manual and added, "As part of the staff, you'll be entitled to two complimentary meals. One when you arrive in the morning and the other before you leave the restaurant at night."

With these instructions delivered, Vikas left Ashua to familiarize himself with his new surroundings, providing him the space to settle into his role at the restaurant.

Ashua carefully observed the staff members working in the restaurant and found them to be friendly and welcoming. Mr. Lalit, the chef, skillfully cooked delicious meals to meet the demands of the customers. Vikas efficiently served the dishes to the patrons who had placed their orders. Varun, the accountant, handled the financial aspects of the restaurant, while Gaurav diligently mopped the floor to maintain cleanliness.

As it was Ashua's first day at work, he made his way to the corner of the kitchen where a pile of dirty dishes was waiting to be cleaned. The area emitted an unpleasant odor, making it challenging for Ashua to stay in one spot for long. However, with time, he grew accustomed to the smell and diligently carried out the task he was assigned.

This was Ashua's first job, and unlike others, he was excited about the opportunity to clean the plates. He firmly believed that no job was less important than another. He had a job to do, and he felt obligated to perform it to the best of his abilities.

While cleaning the dishes, Ashua's mind began to wander. He contemplated, "Today, my job may be washing plates, but it's still a good start. Something is better than nothing. I will work diligently and with dedication, and maybe one day I will have the opportunity to run a place like this. Everyone has to start from scratch, and success doesn't come overnight. I will work my way up, save money, and eventually start something of my own. I refuse to let circumstances control my life. I must earn money and let money work for me. It will take time, so I will enjoy the journey rather than focusing solely on the destination."

This mindset set Ashua miles apart from others. He had a clear vision for his future. While most people were content working for others and making them rich through their hard work, Ashua aspired to work for himself and create wealth. This was just the beginning of his journey.

As minutes turned into hours, Ashua tirelessly cleaned plate after plate. Although his body grew tired, his soul remained invigorated. He continued cleaning until evening, when it was time to close the restaurant for the night.

The people in the restaurant were astonished by the remarkable enthusiasm and dedication with which Ashua worked. After finishing his meal at the restaurant , he left the restaurant, heading towards his brother's place with the hope of getting a good night's sleep, as he was exhausted from his long day.

Taking the bus, Ashua arrived at his brother's residence. As he approached the front door, he heard raised voices and heated arguments coming from inside the house. Ramesh and Meena, his brother and sister-in-law, were engaged in a fierce dispute. It was evident to Ashua that he was the topic of their dispute.

With a mix of trepidation and uncertainty, Ashua cautiously opened the door. Inside, he saw Meena, seething with anger and fury. She wasted no time in making her feelings known. "Think of the devil, and the devil arrives," she spat.

Ashua instantly understood that the situation was far from ideal. Meena bluntly declared, "Listen, Ashua, Ramesh brought you here without consulting me, but I can't allow you to stay any longer. You must leave immediately and let us have peace."

Ashua remained silent, absorbing Meena's words. He stood in the corner of the room, feeling numb and unsure of what to do or say. A sudden rumble of thunder outside signaled the arrival of a heavy rainstorm.

The revelation that his own brother didn't want him to stay hit Ashua like a bolt of lightning. He was unprepared for such rejection. Ramesh, who stood motionless throughout the confrontation, seemed like a coward, only concerned about his own interests. The man inside him was dead. Ashua had misjudged both his brother and his wife. Regret filled his heart as he realized he should never have come to the city with Ramesh.

Amidst the turmoil, Ashua found solace in the thought that Babaji, their father, was spared from witnessing this family drama. The sight would have devastated him. Slowly, Ashua gathered his belongings and stepped outside into the pouring rain. Before leaving the premises, he cast one last glance at Ramesh, who remained silent, consumed by his own shame. The man Ashua once looked up to had lost his sense of responsibility.

It was pouring heavily, and Ashua found himself wandering the dark streets, searching for shelter. Charbattia was not a safe place, especially during the night. Ashua could have fallen victim to robbery or even worse. Yet, Ramesh remained mute. The man Ashua believed his brother to be had perished within him.

After walking for some time, Ashua stumbled upon a tiny, open shed. Stray dogs of various sizes and colors lay sleeping all around it. He placed his bag on the ground and settled himself on the wet floor of the shed, seeking refuge from the rain.

Overwhelmed by the events that had unfolded, Ashua buried his head in his folded arms and began sobbing uncontrollably. However, there was no one to hear his cries. As his tears fell, the homeless dogs around him grew restless and joined in with their own howls. In that moment, Ashua felt a like the stray dogs that were beside him—lonely and worthless. Nobody wanted them, not even his own brother.

Summary

Trust none but yourself.

Chapter 3

*I*t had been a long and seemingly eternal night for Ashua. He anxiously awaited the break of dawn, and each passing minute felt like hours. Just like the dogs surrounding him, he had his tail between his legs, feeling abandoned and uncared for in the harsh, wintry night.

Throughout the night, Ashua wept like a child, overwhelmed by the uncertainty of his future. He regretted his decision to come to Charbattia and realized he had placed his trust in the wrong person. The harsh winds blew relentlessly, fueling thoughts of returning to his village, Magaon.

After hours of weeping and sulking, exhaustion took over, and Ashua closed his eyes, drifting into a deep sleep. In the midst of his slumber, the weather suddenly changed. The rain ceased, and the gusts of wind that had been blowing frantically subsided. It was in this moment that an unexpected visitor appeared before him once again—the hermit, who was always there for Ashua. With a mysterious smile, the hermit looked straight at Ashua and spoke in a hasty manner, "You are not a loser, Ashua. Today may not be your day, but life is ever-changing. It ebbs and flows, just like the waves in the sea. You must fight your way up and not let one incident dictate your entire life. Losers are those who give up, and you, Ashua, are no quitter. You cannot let circumstances control you. Giving up is never an option for those who aspire to achieve great things in life. Think about your father, who sent you to this city with so much hope and expectations. You cannot afford to disappoint him, can you? Be brave, fight against all odds, and emerge as a true winner. So, get up, Ashua, and shine."

And after uttering those kind and inspiring words, the wise man vanished as swiftly as he had appeared. Suddenly, Ashua opened his eyes in astonishment, only to find himself surrounded by the lazy dogs who had become his only companions. It was just a dream, but Ashua knew what he had to do. The hermit had guided him towards the right path at the right time, but he had to wait until dawn as darkness still prevailed.

The next morning, Ashua shivered in the cold aftermath of the rainfall. As he opened his eyes, he was taken aback by the scenes unfolding around the shed where he had taken refuge.

People were taking their regular morning walks, and students carried their bags on their shoulders, heading to school. The cars swiftly moved along the road, reminding him that he was alive and kicking. The street was bustling with life.

Gathering all his strength, Ashua rose to his feet and bought some food from a nearby shop using the money Babuji had given him. As he ate, he humbly shared a portion of his food with the dogs, his friends in this time of need, as a token of appreciation for their companionship. They had been there for him when the world had turned its back on him. He would never forget this night.

The sun began to bathe the surroundings in its warm glow. It was a new day, the start of something new. Ashua went to a public restroom, changed his clothes, and prepared for work. He caught the bus to "DARBAR" and arrived on time, ready to face the challenges ahead.

Ashua arrived at the restaurant and immediately began working diligently. Everyone could sense that something was different about him. He appeared troubled and lost in his own thoughts. Though no one knew the exact reason, they could tell that Ashua was going through something difficult.

Homeless and penniless, Ashua had no place to stay and no means to survive in this harsh and unforgiving city. Yet, he remained silent and continued to work. He longed to talk to someone, but he didn't know who to reach out to. He had no friends in the city, and he felt utterly alone and helpless.

Vikas, who had been observing Ashua from a distance, couldn't resist approaching him. Ashua was busy with his assigned task of dishwashing when Vikas walked up to him. With a sympathetic look, Vikas asked, "Ashua, are you alright?"

Ashua looked up at Vikas with eyes filled with helplessness. Tears welled up in his eyes as he confided, "Vikas, something drastic happened last night."

Not knowing what had transpired, Vikas asked, "What happened to you, my friend?"

Ashua replied, his voice trembling, "Vikas, I was thrown out of my brother's house last night. I have nowhere to go, and I have no money. My own brother has abandoned me. I feel unwanted and worthless. I've become a scavenger in this city. Maybe I shouldn't have come here."

Hearing Ashua's heartbreaking story, Vikas's heart melted with compassion. Despite facing his own challenges, he had an offer that could potentially change Ashua's destiny.

Vikas said, "If you want, you can stay with me. I live in a nearby rented apartment, and I live alone. It gets lonely at times, and I would appreciate your company. We can split the rent, making it economically feasible for both of us."

It is said that God comes in many forms to help those in need, and in this moment, Vikas became Ashua's God-sent savior. However, Ashua was hesitant to accept the offer. He didn't trust anyone in the city, especially a stranger like Vikas. He replied, "I don't have any money right now. I will find a place for myself."

Vikas was taken aback by Ashua's response, but he was determined to help him. He reassured Ashua, saying, "Don't worry about money for now. You'll have money once you receive your salary. Until then, I will take care of things."

With these words, the dark clouds that had enveloped Ashua began to dissipate. He finally had a place to stay and had found a friend, perhaps a friend for a lifetime. In the evening after work Ashua gathered his belongings and settled them in the small room provided by Vikas. Over time, their friendship would only grow stronger.

Every day, Ashua arrived at work with a sense of purpose. He fulfilled his duties to the best of his ability, but he also observed and absorbed everything happening around him in the restaurant. With hawk like keen eyes, he watched the head chef, as he prepared the food, carefully noting the ingredients used in each dish. He observed Vikas serving the meals to the delighted customers, and he even kept a close watch on Mr. Seth, the manager, to understand how the restaurant was being run. Like an eagle soaring above the clouds, Ashua yearned to rise above everyone and excel, for which he knew he needed to learn all the tricks of the trade.

Ashua often engaged himself in friendly conversations with the accountant and other staff members, offering his assistance whenever needed. Gradually, everyone began liking Ashua and seeking his help from time to time, and Ashua eagerly lent a hand with their duties.

In the process, it was Ashua who was gaining valuable knowledge and insights into the various aspects of running a restaurant. Ashua was determined to grasp every detail and understand how the entire operation functioned.

Ashua's aspirations extended beyond mere dishwashing. As time went by, significant changes occurred within the restaurant. Weeks turned into months, and Ashua found himself growing closer to everyone on the team. He frequently approached Mr. Lalit, the head chef, to observe his cooking techniques. Occasionally, Mr. Lalit allowed Ashua to cook under his watchful eyes. During one such interaction, Mr. Lalit shared a crucial lesson with Ashua: cooking is all about ratios and proportions. The right balance of ingredients gives a dish its perfect taste. For example, if you add one teaspoon of sugar to one cup of water, then for two cups of water, you should use two teaspoons of sugar.

Curious about Mr. Lalit's perspective, Ashua once asked him, "Lalit, what do you enjoy most about this job?"

With a smile, Lalit replied, "The best part of this job is, of course, the paychecks we receive at the end of the month. However, it's priceless when customers appreciate the meals I prepare. Sometimes, they even tip me for my efforts, and that makes it all worthwhile."

Mr. Lalit, a devoted family man, had two sons whom he wanted to provide with a good education. He worked tirelessly with the hope that his sons would have better opportunities in life and pursue careers as engineers. Though he may not have been entirely satisfied with his own job, he cherished a dream for his children's future. From noon until dusk, he labored diligently to support his family and fulfill his aspirations for his sons.

In Ashua Lalit saw a part of himself when he was young. He was filled with enthusiasm and had a deep desire to learn and that's what kept him motivated all the time. Ashua always had a sense of purpose and he was on a mission and only time will tell if would be successful in his endeavour.

It had taken more than two years for Ashua to have perfected the art of communication at the restaurant. After making a lot of friends and living a fairly decent life everything was going just fine for Ashua.

Many seasons had gone by and it was time for the rainy season to throw its tantrums.

One morning the weather was overcast, it was pouring outside and everyone had come to the restaurant but Mr. Lalit the head chef was not present. The restaurant had opened and footfall was expected as usual at the restaurant.

Mr.Seth came to the kitchen with a white face. He wore a worried look that told a story and it was not going to be good. He had a frown on his brow. He looked very worried.

Mr. Seth with a stern look on his face told everybody, "Gentlemen we have a problem today."

Everyone looked at each other and were wondering what the hell must have happened.

Mr. Seth continued "Mr. Lalit will not be able to join us at the restaurant today. He is down with a fever. We have no substitute for him today. Now, who will do the cooking today."

Dependency on one person is not good Mr. Seth learns it the hard way.

There was complete silence in the kitchen. Everyone became edgy but out of nowhere the silence was broken by a soft voice coming from the corner of the kitchen. The voice was of none other than that Ashua.

"I can do the cooking today as Mr. Lalit is not here Mr. Seth," said Ashua.

Mr. Seth looked straight at Ashua with those piercing eyes and thought for a moment and said two simple words that would change Ashuas' life forever "OK Ashua".

Mr. Seth like all good managers was always watching his staff like a hawk from his office. He knew what each of them was capable of doing and he had a keen eye on Ashua from the time he had joined the restaurant. He saw the fire in Ashua, and how hard he was working.

He would often see Ashua assisting Mr. Lalit in the kitchen, so he knew that Ashua would not disappoint him.

Now, this was the testing time for Ashua. Ashua had made a promise and now he must deliver.

As the crowd began to swell the place and there were people everywhere, Ashua began to spread his magic. Ashua was a bit nervous in the beginning but as he saw the customers bite into the cuisine his nervousness turned to pleasure. He was enjoying each dish he was preparing and was looking forward to the reaction of his customers.

He prepared dish after dish with utmost perfection. People were leaving the restaurant with big

smiles and the tips the waiters were getting were never better.

It was a day worth remembering for Ashua.

In the evening Mr. Seth came to Ashua and said the words that made Ashua's soul laudable. He said with excitement "Ashua my boy, I am proud of you. You did a wonderful job tonight and we will see about your increment. But from now onwards you will assist Lalit in the kitchen."

Ashua had never been this proud of himself. He felt that he had won a battle and that his hard work had paid off. Never before had Ashua been praised for his efforts but today was his day.

Now Ashua had something to look forward to. He knew his Life's purpose.

He was not just made to raise goats in Magaon his village or wash plates but he was born to cook. He was now the assistant cook at "DARBAR".

Ashua did not just add ingredients to the cuisines he prepared. He cooked them delicately with love

and care and maybe that made each of them special.

It was late at night and the restaurant was closing.

Ashua was very tired after the Herculesous effort he had put in.

As he was leaving for his adobe Vikas told Ashua that he was going to Lalits' house to see how Lalit was doing. Lalit had never taken leave from the restaurant from the time he had joined "DARBAR" so Vikas was a bit worried. He asked Ashua if he would join him to which Ashua promptly agreed.

They together took the bus that would take them to Lalits' house. Both Vikas and Ashua were wondering what must have happened to Lalit. They did not talk much during the ride. Soon the bus reached the house of Mr. Lalit. Ashua and Vikas got off the bus. The head chef's house was close to the bus stand and as they approached his house they heard a faint sounds coming from Lalit's apartment. As they got closer to his house the sounds became clear. There were the sounds of music coming from inside the house of Mr. Lalit. This bewildered Ashua. Ashua looked at Vikas in amusement. Vikas not knowing what was happening inside the house looked at Ashua smiling.

Not knowing what was happening Ashua knocked at the door he did not know what to expect. Soon the door opened and look who opened the door. Lalit was at the door with a can of beer in his hand and he started laughing vociferously on seeing his friends from the restaurant. It did not take long for newly arrived guests to realize that there was a party going on inside the house.

Lalit said laughing loudly "Buddiesit is my son's birthday today so I decided to spend my time with my

Family. Now that you have come please join us." Now everyone was laughing.

Ashua and Vikas entered the house and the spectacle they saw was a very pleasant one. The kids were running everywhere. The music was playing loudly and meals were being served at the table. Everyone was having a great time.

Seeing all this Ashua started to remember his own family. Family is such an important part of our lives.

We earn paychecks only because we want our families to a lead good life. A family consists of many individuals and each individual is important. If a single member of the family gets sad the sadness is transmitted to all the members equally. Family can bring you joy like no other. But it was his brother that had inflected him a wound that was hard to heal.

Seeing all the things around him made Ashua feel that he too should get married and start a family.

As it was getting late the guests had their dinner which had been cooked by Lalit and they rush to their abode as it was past midnight.

Summary
To succeed observe everybody silently and master your craft slowly.

Chapter 4

Working at the restaurant was a demanding task for Ashua, as he took on most of the cooking responsibilities while Lalit guided him through the process. Ashua held Lalit in high regard, considering him his mentor, and treated him with utmost respect, often addressing him as "Ustad."

With each passing day, Ashua honed his skills at work, constantly striving for perfection. Though perfection is difficult to achieve, Ashua was determined to improve himself each passing day.. He had developed his own unique style of cooking. The dishes he prepared started gaining popularity, drawing more people to the restaurant. Ashua had successfully established himself as a renowned chef at "DARBAR."

Despite lacking the formal education he desired back home, Ashua found solace in constant experimentation with different cuisines. He would mix and match ingredients until new and innovative dishes were born. In his eyes, he saw himself as an artist, not just a chef. He aimed to provide his customers with a dining experience unlike any other. Word of mouth spread throughout Charbattia, and people flocked to "DARBAR," associating the name Ashua with excellence.

Over time, Ashua began earning a decent income. He dutifully sent a portion of his earnings back home to Babuji, but he also made it a point to save most of his money. Ashua understood the importance of saving, knowing that unforeseen circumstances could strike at any moment. Saving money was a virtue he believed everyone should cultivate.

Having spent three years at "DARBAR," Ashua had learned invaluable lessons and honed his cooking skills to perfection. However, he knew that it was time to move beyond his apprenticeship and embark on a new journey. Deep within, he harbored secret plans that he kept hidden from everyone, patiently awaiting the right moment to execute them.

As time passed, Ashua found it increasingly challenging to stay motivated. He grew weary of working for others and contemplated the limitations of making his masters wealthier. A yearning for something fresh and new started to consume him. It was during this period that he nurtured a secret desire to establish his own business.

Ashua immersed himself in deep contemplation, exploring various business models and ideas that could work for him. He pondered how these ideas could work for him, seeking an opportunity that would ignite his passion. Yet, none of the ideas seemed enticing enough to pursue.

In his belief that the universe always has a place for everyone, Ashua remained patient, knowing that his time would come. He held onto two guiding principles: working hard and working smart, trusting that the universe would provide the guidance he needed. Like a stork, patiently waiting for the right time, Ashua fixed his gaze upon the horizon, waiting for the right opportunity to unfold.

One cold wintry evening, while sitting alone in his room, Ashua was suddenly struck by a memory. He recalled a conversation with Vikas from the previous day when he mentioned an old food truck was for sale. This news sparked a revelation in Ashua's mind. He saw the tremendous potential of food trucks—a concept that was still relatively new in the city. Realizing that this could be a life-changing opportunity, Ashua made up his mind to buy it.

Despite not having the necessary funds, he knew he had to take a leap of faith. The following day, at the restaurant, Ashua approached Vikas quietly and whispered, "Vikas, you mentioned someone selling their old food truck."

Curious, Vikas asked, "Yes, but why do you ask?"

With determination in his voice, Ashua replied, "I'm interested in buying it."

Vikas was taken aback by Ashua's decision and questioned him, "Are you certain about this? Buying a food truck is a big commitment."

Without a moment's hesitation, Ashua affirmed, "Yes, I am sure. I will buy it."

Vikas hastily said, "Tomorrow, I will take you to the owner. His name is Neeraj, and I know him well. We will discuss with him how much he wants for the truck, and if it fits your budget, we can negotiate."

Ashua eagerly wanted to meet Neeraj. He had a sleepless night, thinking all night long about what would happen during his encounter with Neeraj. The next morning, both Ashua and Vikas dressed in their finest business suits went to meet Neeraj. Neeraj was a middle-aged man with a big mustache, and he wore spectacles. Despite having a grim look on his face, he seemed to be a very intelligent person. One thing Ashua had at the back of his mind was, "Why was Neeraj selling his food truck?"

Both parties sat face to face for the negotiation, and there was an air of tension in the room. Both parties wanted to get the better of each other. Ashua wanted the truck as cheap as possible, while Neeraj wanted a fair price for his food truck. They looked into each other's eyes as if some sort of contest was going on. Ashua told Neeraj that if he sold the food truck to him at the right price then he would buy the raw material from Neeraj that was required at food truck and that would benefit Neeraj immensely. Neeraj knew that he was dealing with a tough nut and it was going to be a give and take relationship. It would be a win-win situation for both of them if the deal was cracked. Nothing in life is for free. You give from one hand then only you will receive from the other. There is no free lunch.

After one hour of quick negotiations, Neeraj quoted the final price, saying, "Buddy, I will not sell it for less than 7 lakh rupees." To which Ashua replied, "5 lakh is the right price for your used truck." Ashua knew how to negotiate, and he had set the lowest price for the truck.

Neeraj quickly understood what Ashua was planning, so he said, "No, no, it might be old, but it works just like a new one."

The negotiation carried on for a while and came to an end when Neeraj said, "Okay, I will sell you the truck for 6 lakh rupees, but no less, otherwise, the deal is off."

After pondering for some time, Ashua grew worried. He realized that he might lose this opportunity if he didn't seal the deal now. With a sense of urgency, he agreed and said, "We have a deal, Mr. Neeraj."

Although Ashua knew he was getting the truck at a fair price, he faced a financial challenge—he didn't have the money at hand. Neeraj promptly asked, "When will you provide the payment?"

Needing more time, Ashua sought to buy himself some breathing space and replied, "Give me one month." However, Neeraj responded harshly, "No, I can only give you 15 days. I have another buyer, and if you fail to pay within 15 days, I will sell it to them."

Reluctantly, Ashua agreed to the shortened timeline. Vikas, who had been witnessing the entire episode, was startled when the deal was finalized. He whispered to Ashua softly, "Do you know what you're doing? Do you have this kind of money?"

To this, Ashua replied, "No, but it will come." Ashua had now started to believe in himself.

As Vikas and Ashua left the place, the weather grew overcast once again, hinting at an impending rainstorm.

Vikas contemplated, "What is wrong with this boy? Just when everything seemed to be going right for him, he does something foolish to jeopardize his own life and career." However, Ashua knew what he was doing; he understood the need to take risks in order to achieve something worthwhile. No pain, no gain. Deep in thought, he evaluated his finances. After working hard in the restaurant, he had managed to save three lakh rupees, but he needed an additional three lakh rupees to purchase the food truck. He couldn't let a mere amount of three lakh rupees stand between him and his dream.

Determined to raise the money, Ashua reached out to a few friends, but to no avail. Despite offering them the opportunity to become partners in his venture, no one was willing to invest in Ashua's aspirations.

What hurt Ashua the most was not just the lack of financial support, but that no one had faith in him or his idea. Feeling alone in the world with no one believing in him, Ashua had to rely solely on his own belief in himself.

While many would give up when the world turned its back on them,but Ashua was no quitter. He was a fighter, determined not to give up even when faced with tough circumstances. Those were testing days for Ashua, and he thought deeply about his options. Finally, he approached Vikas with the hope of borrowing some money. Reluctantly, Vikas agreed to lend Ashua one lakh rupees on the condition that he becomes a partner in the venture. Ashua gladly accepted, seeing this as an opportunity to strengthen their friendship and work together towards their dreams.

In Vikas, Ashua saw a loyal, hard-working person, and he trusted him to be a valuable collaborator in his venture. However, despite this support, the problem of not having enough money to buy the food truck persisted. Ashua explored every avenue, but all his efforts were in vain. With only two days left to deposit the money, Ashua felt utterly helpless. He had exhausted all his resources and had lost hope of finding a way to arrange the required funds. His dream was shattered, and he felt like a disappointed soul, wondering if he had asked too much from life.

One last time Ashua got off the chair knelt on the floor of his room and closed his eyes and prayed to the almighty with his heart filled with hope and desire that his prayers will be answered. He remembered the hermit from the past, whom he was blessed to have seen. He closed his eyes and prayed "O God please help me, you are my only hope. I don't have the money that is required to buy the food truck. Bless me and help me to arrange the funds " And then he opened his eyes. He had faith in the almighty and he believed in himself. He knew that his prayers will be answered. Faith and hope can keep any dream alive. As the deadline was getting closer and closer. Ashua was returning home at night after work deeply engrossed in his thought. Out of the blue he heard a scream. At first, he thought it was his wild imagination but as the screams got louder and louder he turned towards the direction where the voices were coming from. There he saw a woman draped in a red saree surrounded by goons. This sight bewildered him. The woman was a middle-aged beautiful lady and she seemed to be coming from some social gathering. She was wearing beautiful clothes and some fancy jewelry and she was petrified. Her scream was deafening. She was asking for help. But no one came to her recuse. One goon held a knife in front of her and was asking the woman to remove the jewelry she was wearing.

On seeing this woman in trouble Ashua rushed to the spot. Without giving a thought he picked a big stone that was the only weapon available in the vicinity. And he quickly hit the man holding the knife on his right shoulder. The other goons surrounded Ashua, but Ashua bravely held his ground. Now it was a game of courage and mind. Ashua picked a goon that seemed to be the weakest among them and kept hitting him furiously with the stone. Every blow was making him bleed. Seeing this happening to their companion the other goons fled. Running as fast as they could from this madman. After all the goons had fled the spot Ashua gave a sign of relief but he was exhausted. He lay on the ground and closed his eyes for a while. After a few seconds, he opened his eyes and saw that the lady whom he had just saved was wiping the dust from his face gently with the corner of her saree. She seemed worried for this stranger who had risked his life for hers. "Are you alright?" she said with a face filled with gratitude.

"Yes "replied Ashua.

Ashua got up exhausted as he was drained of all his energy and stood still for some time. The lady was humbled by the action of this young stranger. The lady said softly with a voice filled with gratitude "THANK YOU, young man. You saved me from those goons. You have been a lifesaver and I can't thank you enough." "What is your name young man? "she continued.

Ashua said humbly " My name is Ashua ma'am". There was an awkward silence for some time no one spoke a word. The lady was in awe of this person who had just saved her life. This lady was short of words for the courage displayed by Ashua. The lady broke the silence and introduced herself and said "My name is Sita. I was returning from an engagement ceremony of a relative when these goons tried to rob me. If you had not come to my recuse things would have taken a very rough turn. You are the bravest person I have ever met. Thank you again for saving my life". Ashua said humbly not realizing that this type of bravery was not common in the city " Don't embarrass me ma'am I was just doing what anybody else would do." Sita said with those thankful beautiful black eyes " I don't know how to show my appreciation but I have a humble request for you. Kindly come with me to my house I want you to meet my husband".

Ashua readily agreed to drop her at her house as he did not want to leave her alone after the incident in this part of the city. After a few blocks away they reached Sita's house. It was a huge bungalow with a big iron gate at the entrance. Sita went inside her house with Ashua and got some water for him. Soon she was joined by her kids and husband. Sita told her husband Sumit in detail how Ashua had saved her from the goons. Her two kids were also listening. They were awestruck. They saw Ashua in a different light. He bacame their hero. All heroes don't wear a cape and a real hero was right there in front of them. A person can become a hero through his act of courage and bravery and he doesn't have to have superpowers as some think. Sumit was very grateful as Ashua had saved his wife. His heart was filled with a desire to help Ashua in some way. So Sumit asked Ashua "Young man you have saved us from a lot of trouble and I am very grateful for that. Please tell me how can I repay you as a token of appreciation." Ashua was initially hesitant to ask Sumit for a favor. As Sumit continued "I am a banker and I work at the KNSB bank which is one of the best banks in the city. Tell me if can I help you in some way." The word bank had a ring to it. It got Ashua thinking.

Ashua explained to Sumit in great detail his plans to embark on a business venture and his urgent need for funds to purchase a food truck. With a glimmer of hope, he inquired whether it would be possible to obtain a loan from Sumit's bank. Without hesitation, Sumit enthusiastically agreed to assist Ashua and requested him to visit the bank with the necessary documents. He assured Ashua that he would personally help him secure the loan he required. This was precisely the breakthrough Ashua had been hoping for.

After spending sometime with the family, Ashua returned to his room where Vikas awaited him. Eagerly, he recounted the entire episode to Vikas, who was astounded by what he had just heard. With admiration and sincerity, Vikas remarked, "God has truly been kind to you, my friend. You are not only courageous but also blessed with good fortune."

In response, Ashua humbly shook his head, acknowledging the fact that -fortune favors the brave. The turn of events had further reinforced his belief that taking risks and facing challenges can lead to remarkable opportunities. With newfound hope and gratitude, Ashua eagerly prepared himself for the next step in his journey, guided by the belief that his determination and bravery would continue to pave the way toward his dreams and aspirations.

Summary
Fortune favors the brave and the daring.

Chapter 5

The next day, Ashua went to the bank with Vikas, and Sumit anxiously awaited his arrival. By chance, something unexpected happened—Sumit turned out to be the bank manager. Fortune does favors the brave at times.

As Ashua entered the bank, all eyes were glued to him. The news of his brave endeavor must have spread quickly, as everyone passed him big smiles while he made his way slowly towards the branch manager's cabin.

Ashua comfortably sat down in the manager's cabin and waited. After completing all the formalities at the bank, he was granted a loan of 3 Lakhs Rupees. Although not a very large amount, it was enough to keep Ashua's dreams alive. He was well aware that the loan he had just secured was not his to keep; it had to be repaid within a certain period. Nevertheless, he was elated to have the loan as it provided him with a chance to fulfill his desires.

With the money he needed to buy the food truck in his possession, Ashua promptly went to Neeraj and handed him the money, which Neeraj accepted gladly. Both negotiators were happy with the deal they had just finalized.

Neeraj handed over the keys to the food truck to Ashua—a moment he would never forget. It was a proud moment for him, as he had never imagined he would come this close to starting his own business so quickly. His dreams were beginning to take shape, but he knew there was still a long way to go. Success, as wise people say, is a never-ending path. Just when you think you have succeeded, you come to the sudden realization that there is more to achieve.

As Ashua proudly held the keys to the food truck, a sudden burden settled upon him. He had made his first investment and now had to ensure it was worth it—a responsibility he willingly accepted.

Now, the truck needed a name. After much deliberation, Ashua decided to call it "SUDHA," meaning "pure." The food truck was taken to the garage for repairs and repainted all white with a hint of orange. Its exteriors were redone to make it look new and appealing. The name "SUDHA" was deliberately engraved on the front portion. It took Ashua time and money to renovate the truck, but it was worth it.

The name of the food truck, "SUDHA," meaning "pure," reflected Ashua's aspirations. He aimed to serve the best dishes in town at the best prices. It would be a value-for-money food truck, and the quality of the food would be of the highest order. Now it was time to prepare the menu card, and Ashua and Vikas decided it had to be special. The duo brainstormed extensively about the type of food they would sell from the truck to make them stand out in this fiercely competitive market.

If they were to succeed in the market, their cuisine had to be different from what other vendors were selling. Ashua knew that to stand out from the crowd, they needed to be unique. Thus, he began creating a menu card that would have a distinct look and offer cuisines that were not available anywhere else in the city. He planned to bring dishes from different places and cook them in his own style.

Ashua started experimenting with the cuisines he intended to sell. He aimed to create a perfect menu card, knowing that perfection required practice. Devoting countless hours, he honed his skills in creating dishes that would captivate the taste buds of anyone who tried them. Drawing from his experience at the DARBAR, he mixed and matched ingredients to invent new culinary creations.

After hours of experimentation, Ashua crafted a flawless menu. It featured incredible cuisines that would tantalize the palates of those who indulged in them. Ashua was confident that people would love the food, but he had to wait for the right moment.

With the menu finalized, Ashua made the difficult decision to quit his job at the DARBAR. It was an emotional farewell as the restaurant had played a significant role in shaping him into the person he had become. At "DARBAR," he had been a dedicated student, learning valuable lessons that he knew he could never fully repay. Saying goodbye to the restaurant was bittersweet, with the staff bidding farewell and wishing him success in his new venture. They knew that Ashua's absence would leave a void that could never be filled. His stories of hard work and determination would echo through the restaurant's corridors forever. It was a tearful departure, as everyone held a deep affection for him.

However, life moves on, and so did Ashua. In order to achieve something, one must be willing to let go of things that may be important. Sacrifices must be made, and stepping out of one's comfort zone is essential to fulfill dreams.

Within a few days, Ashua purchased the necessary raw materials and other supplies for the food truck. As he turned on the engine, the wheels of SUDHA began to roll. It marked the beginning of a new adventure—a journey where Ashua had the pleasure of working for himself, which seemed unfamiliar to Vikas, his friend and business partner. Throughout his life, Vikas had always worked for others, and now he was venturing into the realm of self-employment.

The risks that Ashua had taken were enormous, but they were risks that had to be taken at some point in time. To achieve something in life, one must step out of their shell and leave their comfort zone. Only then can an ordinary person accomplish extraordinary things. It requires risking a stable, ordinary life and taking a gamble to access an extraordinary one.

Before starting the engine, Ashua closed his eyes and immersed himself in deep prayer. Humbly, he prayed for good luck and fortune to pave his way. He prayed for success in his new business venture and to make his father proud. He recalled the hermit he had encountered in an unlikely event in his village and sought his blessings. The outcome of heartfelt prayers is yet to be seen, as they are heard and answered in their own time.

In business, it is not just hard work that matters; luck also plays a crucial role. Great ideas and ample capital may not be enough if luck is not on your side. Businesses thrive when the right people with the right ideas are present at the right place and time. And for this winning combination, Lady Luck must be on your side.

Ashua and Vikas, Ashua's business partner, set out with the food truck to one of the busiest streets in the city called Melrose Street. It was a highly competitive location, but Ashua wanted to compete with the best and reap greater profits. The street was like an ocean of people, with individuals from all walks of life, each one a potential customer in Ashua and Vikas' eyes. It was a street lined with numerous office buildings, where the hungry, hard-working employees would take a break from their busy schedules to grab a bite from one of the food trucks during lunchtime.

It wouldn't be easy, as many people had already made reservations at other food outlets. For a newcomer like Ashua, it posed a challenging task ahead.

It was a beautiful afternoon as Ashua parked his food truck on the corner of the street, ready to serve customers during the lunch break. After a few hours of waiting, people started coming out of their offices to grab lunch from various food joints on the busy street. The atmosphere resembled a swarm of bees, with people bustling around, engrossed in their conversations. These individuals hailed from different parts of the town, dressed in varied attire and speaking different dialects, highlighting the cosmopolitan nature of the place.

Despite the crowd, no one seemed to notice the new food truck that had just arrived at the corner. People already had their reservations at other food joints. Unfortunately, the attention of potential customers remained elusive.

Ashua anxiously waited for the moment when someone would approach his food truck, hoping that others would follow suit. However, the wait became increasingly long. From noon until night, no one came to their food truck. This disappointing pattern continued for three consecutive days. Despite parking their truck at the busy street corner, no one bothered to check it out. The established food vendors seemed to attract all the customers, leaving Ashua and Vikas feeling uncertain and discouraged. They were at a loss for what to do next and hoped that the next day would bring a change in fortune, but their luck didn't seem to improve.

On the fourth day, Ashua and Vikas decided to roll their food truck back home. They knew it was time for introspection. With not a single item sold, Vikas felt deeply disappointed and worried about his future. He feared having to find another job if things continued like this.

However, Ashua had a different mindset. Instead of dwelling on the problems, he focused on finding a solution. He realized that most of their potential customers were office-goers, who were conscious about saving money. Ashua brainstormed and came to a conclusion: he needed to entice customers with an offer they couldn't resist.

As the raw materials were approaching their expiration date, Ashua devised a brilliant idea – an offer that said, "ONE MEAL FREE WITH EVERY MEAL." This offer would attract customers to their food truck, even though it wouldn't result in immediate profits. The primary goal was to pull a crowd and get noticed.

The next day, Ashua created a flyer featuring the enticing offer – "ONE MEAL FREE WITH EVERY MEAL." This catchy promotion had the potential to draw customers in, even if it meant they wouldn't make a significant profit at first.

Ashua reached Melrose Street. The street was packed with people. Ashua parked his food truck hoping that this day would be his day. All the other food trucks were also lined up waiting for customers. Ashua looked up toward the blue sky and prayed for a while. As he waited he saw a little girl. She seemed hungry. Ashua went up to her and said "What's your name child". She said softly "Riddhi". Ashua asked her "Do you want to eat anything". Riddhi was startled.

Ashua said, "It is free for you today. You don't need to pay me". Riddhi smiled and said, "Yes, thank you". So Ashua made his first meal at SUDHA FOOD TRUCK. He made it with the same enthusiasm and gave it to Riddhi. As soon as Riddhi took the first bite of it the magic happened.

Ashua was observing her closely and as her facial expressions were changing he knew she loved the food. After she had finished her meal she hesitantly went to Ashua and said "The food was lovely. I have never had such a delicious meal before can you pack one more meal. I will pay you for it". Ashua was a bit surprised and asked her "Are you still hungry". To this Riddhi replied, " I have an elder sister at home and I want you to pack a meal for her too. I know she will be very happy to eat this kind of food". Ashua packed a meal for her sister for which she happily paid. Ashua thought it was a good way to begin the day. He gave a meal free and was paid for the next meal. Riddhi said "Bye".

After placing the flyer in front of the food truck, Ashua eagerly awaited the lunch hour. As the lunch hour closed in, office workers began to pour out onto the street in search of a meal to fulfill their stomach. This time they noticed the flyer promoting a free meal with every purchase at Sudha food truck.

Curiosity piqued, some people decided to give this new venture a try. As they took their first bites, they were pleasantly surprised by the delicious flavors. The food was so satisfying that many customers found themselves craving more. Some even requested to have their meals packed for their family members at home. Word quickly spread, and the order list started growing longer and longer.

Ashua and Vikas worked tirelessly to keep up with the increasing demand. Ashua skillfully cooked the meals, while Vikas efficiently served the customers. However, as the crowd swelled and the orders poured in, they eventually ran out of raw materials and had to close the truck for the day.

Despite the initial challenges, Ashua's unique offer had attracted customers and left them wanting more. The success of that day gave them hope for the future and motivated them to keep pushing forward.

In the evening after work Ashua and Vikas did the accounting for the day. They counted the money they had earned. Ashua and Vikas, despite the recognition and positive response from customers, were disappointed when they counted the day's earnings. The realization struck them that the profits were not as substantial as they had hoped. Giving a free meal with every purchase had impacted their profitability.

As they stared at the money and calculated their meager profit, a sense of concern washed over both Ashua and Vikas. They knew that their current strategy was not sustainable in the long run. They needed to rethink their approach and find ways to increase their profits.

Deep in thought, they brainstormed ideas to broaden their revenue streams. They considered various possibilities, such as introducing additional menu items that could be sold at a higher price point, offering catering services for events, or even exploring partnerships with local businesses.

Vikas told Ashua with concern "We have to stop this free meal thing it is eating away our profits". Ashua also knew this he needed to come up with a different plan. He needed to do something different and quickly. So Ashua came up with a different stragy.

He told "Vikas don't worry we will not give free meals from tomorrow but we will give discounts. They will be like rewards. If a person orders more than one meal we will give him a 10 percent discount and if a person orders four or more meals we will give him a 30 percent discount. This will draw people to our food truck. But we have to keep in mind we don't have to degrade the quality of our food and we will still serve the best food in the street."

The next day Ashua and Vikas set out to Melrose Street with great enthusiasm hoping for the best. The ply card was all prepared with a bold font telling what the SUDHA food truck was offering today to its valuable customers. They set up their food truck at the same place as before and put the ply card in front of their food truck so that people could have a good glance at it and then they waited. Today Ashua brought more raw materials for his dishes than yesterday. He had doubled his raw material so that he could double the meals.

Before he would start his day Ashua saw a man walking in the street he seemed old and weak. He was wearing a worn-out overcoat and was struggling to walk. He seemed poor and hungry. Ashua went up to him and humbly offered him a meal. The old man glanced at Ashua with suspicion, reluctant to take the meal.

Ashua said smilingly, "Don't worry take this meal you need not pay me".

Seeing this generosity come from a stranger seemed strange to this old man. But he took the meal and after munching the meal he blessed Ashua with his wrinkled hands and said softly " May god fulfill all your desires young man and left the place with a full belly.

This practice would become a ritual for Ashua. Every day Ashua would feed a hungry person, after which he would begin to sell his stuff. Sharing is caring. If you want to receive you should first be willing to give. The universe helps those people who care and help others.

Ashua held strongly to the belief that if you feed one hungry soul many other hungry people will come to you and pay you for it.

After some anxious moments on the street, it was lunch time and people began to flock toward the Sudha Food Truck. The crowd began to grow larger and larger at their truck. Not only was the food good but they were also giving a discount which these people could not resist. The word had spread across the street that the new food truck was delivering special food at a great price. It was a value-for-money venture and people loved it.

Soon the crowd at their food truck began to swell. Different types of people from all paths of life were visiting Ashua's food truck.

As days passed by a remarkable thing began to happen at the food truck the lower staff members of the offices were enjoying the meals with their bosses. The bosses and their staff members were mesmerized by the food Ashua prepared diligently.

Soon as the days went by other food joints were rattled by this new food truck that had just come and had eaten up part of their businesses. They were finding it hard to retain their clients.

As SUDHA Food Truck continued to thrive, other food joints in the area grew increasingly desperate. Some started offering discounts, while others focused on improving the quality of their dishes, all in an attempt to compete with Ashua and break the spell he had cast.

However, Ashua and Vikas remained undeterred and enjoyed the fruits of their success. With each passing day, their cash register grew larger, and they found themselves accumulating wealth at an unprecedented rate. Ashua could now send substantial amounts of money to Babuji, fulfilling his dream of making his father proud. Babuji would visit the city, his eyes shining with pride and amazement at Ashua's rapid progress.

Meanwhile, Vikas indulged in the pleasures of his newfound prosperity. He bought fashionable clothes, fulfilling his long-held dreams, and even treated himself to a fancy car. Both Ashua and Vikas were living the life they had always dreamed of.

However, as the crowds flocking to their food truck grew larger, Ashua realized that they needed additional help to handle the increasing demand. With his ambitious nature driving him, Ashua decided it was time to expand their venture. He knew that one food truck alone would not be sufficient to satisfy their growing customer base and fulfill his vision for the future.

Summary

Persistence and patient will make you succeed. Never give up.

Chapter 6

The business was thriving, and money flowed abundantly into their cash drawers. Money has a peculiar nature – when it arrives, it doesn't trickle, it pours. Ashua and Vikas had achieved what they had set out to achieve. Dreamers can become achievers if they work hard and plan diligently. Dreams cease to be dreams when pursued with the right attitude. When dreams transform into reality, people call it luck. And so it was for Ashua and Vikas. Their hard work had paid off, and they had transitioned from dreamers to achievers. Every day, with boundless enthusiasm, Ashua and Vikas drove their food truck to the streets, where a queue of people eagerly awaited a taste of their meals. Their food truck had slowly but steadily gained a reputation as a renowned food joint. Customers from other parts of the town flocked to experience their culinary delights. This new food truck had shaken the foundations of other establishments, leaving them perplexed and unable to compete. How can people say, "What's in a name?" As time passed, replicas of SUDHA began to spring up all over the city. But the original SUDHA stood at its peak. Each day, they sold out, exceeding their wildest expectations. The cash registers were ringing and the sound they were making was loud. Months went by, but Ashua never compromised on the quality of his food, still offering discounts. If he had abandoned these discounts, their profits would have soared even higher. However, greed began to seep into the hearts of Ashua and Vikas. Late one night, after closing up for the day and returning to their new, larger apartment, Vikas expressed his frustration to Ashua. "Buddy, our business is booming. Our sales are skyrocketing. Do we really need to continue these discounts? People will come to us even if we don't offer discounted meals." Ashua knew this question would arise from Vikas one day, as he had contemplated the same dilemma himself.

That night, as Ashua pondered the matter, his thoughts were interrupted by an unexpected visitor.

Looking closely, he could not believe who had come to visit him at this hour. It was the monk he had encountered in his village and he had the same peaceful smile, wearing the same saffron robe. The monk seemed unchanged by time. With great joy and respect, Ashua bowed before him. The monk looked at Ashua and said, "You have accomplished great things, Ashua. You believed in yourself, and now people believe in you. You have achieved more than anyone in your village ever has, and I am very happy for you. However, I must remind you not to let greed consume you. Greed is a vice; it knows no bounds. It leads to deceit, robs you of happiness and finally destroys the soul. Work harder if you want to earn more money, but do not cheat people or resort to shortcuts. You have worked diligently to build a reputation for yourself—do not let it slip away." Ashua listened attentively, taking the monk's words to heart.

He nodded and replied, "You are right, revered monk. I have come a long way, and I must hold onto the values that brought me here. Greed can tarnish everything I have worked for. I will continue to work hard and strive for success, but I will not compromise my integrity or deceive others. Thank you for reminding me of what truly matters."

With a gentle smile, the monk placed a hand on Ashua's shoulder. "I have faith in you, Ashua. You possess a kind heart and the determination to succeed with honor. Stay true to your values, and success will always accompany you."

Suddenly, the monk vanished into thin air, as if he had never been there. Ashua frantically searched for him, calling out in desperation, but the monk was nowhere to be found. He was left with a deep longing to ask the monk his burning questions and seek his blessings. Tears streamed down Ashua's face as he cried out, "Where are you, Holy One?" In that moment, Ashua heard Vikas's voice calling out to him, urging him to wake up. Slowly, Ashua opened his eyes, still disoriented and trying to grasp reality. It took a moment for him to realize that it had all been a dream—a vivid and powerful dream that had touched his soul. Relieved that it was just a dream, Ashua took a deep breath and gathered his thoughts. Although the monk was not physically present, his teachings and guidance remained imprinted in Ashua's heart. The lessons learned and the values instilled would continue to shape Ashua's journey and decisions. With renewed determination, Ashua got up from his bed. The dream had reminded him of the importance of staying true to his values and embracing the path of integrity and hard work. He knew that success was not solely measured by material wealth but by the impact he could make on others' lives. Ashua looked at Vikas, grateful for his presence and support.

Vikas said, "I think you just had a dream, and you were so caught up in it that you started moaning loudly. I was in the next room, and I thought something had happened to you, so I woke you up. Is everything okay?"

Ashua softly replied, "It's all okay, Vikas. I have found the answers to our questions. We will continue running our business in the same way. Nothing will change, but we will now expand. We will purchase more food trucks."

Vikas expressed his concern, "But the discounts we are offering are eating into our profits. Now that we have established ourselves, there is no need for these discounts."

To this, Ashua confidently replied, "Discounts are our unique selling proposition (USP); they attract new customers. If we sell more items, we can make more profit. Our focus will be on increasing sales volume. While the profit on a single item may be lower due to the discounts, with higher sales, our overall profit will be better. In order to achieve this, we will need to hire more people. There are individuals like us, Vikas, who are in need of jobs, have limited resources, and are willing to work hard and we will employ them."

With Ashua taking charge of the decision, the discussion came to an end. Vikas understood that Ashua's perspective was correct, and he respected his authority as the boss.

The next day, on a beautiful afternoon, Ashua and Vikas rolled their food truck wheels to their location on Melrose Street. Ashua felt a sense of happiness and clarity, as his vision had become clear and he no longer had any doubts. It had been a few days since the window to his mind had been dusty and blur, but now he knew exactly what to do.

The journey of success and the pursuit of money can have a profound impact on one's soul. Everybody starts with nothing but dreams, hope, and desires, and as you achieve a little money, you often find yourself wanting more and more. This road is endless.

On that fine sunny afternoon, Ashua set up his food truck on the street as usual and performed his customary prayer. As he looked around with his sharp eyes searching for potential customers, he noticed a little girl who seemed like an angel. Upon closer examination, Ashua realized that he had seen her before—it was Riddhi, the same girl to whom he had given a taste of a free meal on his first day at the job.

Riddhi greeted Ashua with a smile and said, "Hello, how are you?"

Ashua was touched by her sweet voice and replied kindly, "I'm good, my sweet little angel. Did you enjoy the food I gave you the last time?"

Riddhi's smile widened as she responded, "I liked it very much. Your food is great, which is why I brought my sister Bhawana to eat at your food joint."

Ashua looked up and saw Bhawana, Riddhi's sister, standing beside her.

Ashua gazed at Bhawana, temporarily lost in his thoughts. He had never seen such a beautiful girl before. Bhawana had a tall, slim figure, and as her hair swayed in the breeze, she looked even more beautiful. Her dark brown eyes held an innocent charm that captivated Ashua. There was something about her that he couldn't take his eyes off. Truly, beauty lies in the eyes of the beholder.

Vikas, who had been observing Ashua from a distance and seeing a love story unfold, abruptly interrupted Ashua. He said, "Ashua, why don't you serve Bhawana our freshly prepared cucumber sandwich? I'm sure she will like it."

Ashua snapped back to reality and realized he had a chance to interact with Bhawana. He nervously served her the sandwich, feeling a mixture of excitement and apprehension. As Bhawana enjoyed her meal, Ashua wanted to strike up a conversation, but he remained silent. Fear of rejection overshadowed his confidence, and he didn't want to ruin their first meeting. So Ashua stood there, still looking at Bhawana, unable to find the right words to say.

After finishing her meal Bhawana casually got up and went to Ashua to pay for the meal.

Ashua nervously said, "No you are our guest today I cannot charge you for the meal."

But Bhawana was reluctant and said in her soft voice that touched Ashua, "No I will pay for the meal. If you don't take the money I will feel guilty and you don't want that do you. So please take the money".

On saying this she paid for her meal and hurriedly left with Raddhi smiling. Ashua was even more impressed with this act of Bhawana. This is one hell of a lady he thought.

As the day went on, Ashua couldn't get Bhawana out of his mind. Her brown eyes and flowing black hair filled his thoughts. He longed to see her again, but he didn't know where she lived or how to contact her. Throughout the night, restlessness consumed him as he yearned for Bhawana's company.

Our boy was in love. The next day, Ashua eagerly waited for Bhawana or to show up. He couldn't focus on his work or anything else, consumed by the thoughts of seeing Bhawana again. However, the wait only grew longer and longer. Vikas, understanding Ashua's hopeless infatuation, took over the operations at the food truck, trying to help his friend. Ashua's desperation to catch a glimpse of Bhawana intensified. He yearned for any sign of her presence.

One day In the evening as Ashua was standing near his food truck lost in his thoughts and doing nothing he saw someone at a distance. His heart began to pound loudly and he almost lost his breath. A slim tall girl was walking across the street. He could not stop himself and rushed in the direction of this girl without giving a thought. His wait seemed to have ended. He reached the spot where this girl was standing and shouted out loudly "HI! BHAWANA". The puzzled girl slowly turned around and said "Do I know you." Ashua soon realized that it was not Bhawana and he mistakenly assumed someone else for her. Ashua had embarrassed himself and made a laughingstock of himself in front of everyone.

Ashua felt embarrassed and apologized, "Sorry, ma'am, I mistook you for someone else." The girl smiled understandingly, her presence adding a touch of warmth to Ashua's flushed face. She reassured him, "It's okay," and gracefully walked away. Ashua couldn't shake off the unease and restlessness that had settled within him. As days turned into weeks, Bhawana didn't visit the food truck. Ashua began to lose hope of ever seeing her again. He resigned himself to the thought that perhaps she wasn't meant to be a part of his life. It was a bittersweet realization. Ashua had to find a way to let go of the little memories he had of Bhawana, a difficult choice but a necessary one. Controlling his thoughts was a challenge, as emotions are not easily tamed. Bhawana had left an indelible mark on his heart, making it hard for Ashua to forget her.

However, time has a way of healing wounds and soothing the ache of lost connections. A month had passed, and the memories of Bhawana began to fade. Ashua slowly resumed his life, embracing the routines he had before meeting her. He realized that life doesn't grant all the desires of the heart. Sometimes, one must let go and allow time to heal the longing. Ashua moved forward, finding solace in the passage of time.

Summary

Love is blind. Never let lady of your dream go without a fight.

Chapter 7

All was going well for Ashua, and life was getting back on track. He had put Bhawana out of his mind and was enjoying his daily routine.

However, on one unexpected afternoon, everything changed. Ashua was busy working at his food truck when he heard a familiar voice from behind him. Slowly turning his head, he was surprised to see the little angel he had longed to see for so long. She had the same radiant smile, and her gaze was fixed on Ashua.

This time, Ashua was determined not to make a fool of himself. He took a long deep breath, rubbed his eyes, and carefully observed the person before him. It was hard to believe, but it was indeed Riddhi. Ashua felt a surge of anticipation, reminiscent of his teenage years.

Curiously, Ashua glanced around to see if Riddhi was accompanied by anyone. To his disappointment, she was standing alone, exuding an air of independence and confidence.

Ashua kindly requested Riddhi to join him. Though hesitant at first, Riddhi mustered the courage and stood before him. Ashua warmly welcomed her, his heart brimming with affection, but refrained from hugging her.

Placing his hands gently on her shoulders, Ashua spoke, "Hello, my little angel. How are you? What would you like to have today?"

Riddhi's eyes sparkled with delight. She felt a sense of connection with this stranger. Offering a slight nod and a radiant smile, she conveyed her choice.

With joy in his heart, Ashua prepared one of his finest sizzlers for her.

As the sizzlers were sizzling, Ashua began to inquire, seeking to know more about the sisters. He turned to Riddhi and asked, "Where do you live my dear?"

Riddhi responded, "We live near the bus station."

Curiosity piqued, Ashua gently questioned further, "Where is Bhawana? Why didn't she come with you today?"

Riddhi appeared taken aback for a moment but replied, "She has gone to work."

Eager to learn more about Bhawana, Ashua asked timidly, "Where does she work?"

Riddhi revealed, "She works at Hariniwas Colony near the bus station. She is employed by an elderly couple who compensate her for managing their house."

Keeping the conversation flowing, Ashua inquired, "And where are your parents?"

Riddhi sadly shared, "They died a few years ago in a horrific accident," her voice tinged with sorrow as tears welled up in her eyes.

Ashua's heart went out to the orphaned sisters, feeling a mix of empathy and sympathy. Unsure of how to console Riddhi, he mustered the courage to ask the question he had been longing to ask, albeit in a delicate manner. He said softly, "Can I have Bhawana's mobile number?"

A moment of silence hung in the air, and Riddhi felt a twinge of unease. However, Ashua quickly added, "Maybe I can assist her in finding a better job."

The tension eased, and Riddhi's smile returned. She willingly shared Bhawana's number with Ashua. Bhawana and Riddhi had shown incredible resilience, facing adversity with a constant smile on their faces.

Deep admiration and respect for the sisters swelled within Ashua. Their presence ignited a renewed determination within him to live a life without complaints. Everyone faces stumbling blocks in life, but it's the ability to rise and work towards a brighter future what matters.

As the sizzler ceased to sizzle, the ice between Riddhi and Ashua was broken. Riddhi savored the delicious food and bid farewell, leaving Ashua with a heart full of hope and anticipation.

Ashua was on top of the world he had the mobile number of his dream girl who had given him so many sleepless nights.

Ashua could not resist the temptation so at night Ashua got up from his bed sat down on his chair and with a very determined mind took out his phone and typed the number that Riddhi had given him. The bell began to ring at the other end. It was agonizing for Ashua as the bell was ringing and no one was picking up the phone.

Suddenly someone picked up the phone and there was a voice at the other end that sleepily said: "Hello! Who's there?"

Ashua mumbled, "Hi this is Ashua here."

Ashua recognized the voice at the other end and yes this was of Bhawana. Ashuas heart began to pound loudly.

Bhawana hastily said, "Sorry wrong number. I don't know of any Ashua ".

And she hung up the phone. Ashua was restless he did not know what to do next. This girl had altered his life in so many ways and given him sleepless nights. And now she says that she does not know him. It was heartbreaking but the power of love was with Ashua so he called again. The phone rang again and Bhawana was at the other end.

This time Ashua did not waste any time and said "I am Ashua do you remember the food truck where you had come with Riddhi? I am the food truck boy. Riddhi gave me your number."

Bhawana suddenly seemed to remember him.

Bhawana said " Yes, The food truck boy. I remember you. Riddhi told me about you. You have been very kind to us. Sorry! I had forgotten your name."

Ashua on the other end was nervously listening to each word coming out of her mouth. This was for the first time, he was having a conversation with a girl that he had longed to be with.

Ashua paused for a moment and breathing slowly he popped the question.

He said, "Can we meet tomorrow?"

It was a big deal for Ashua as he had never asked any girl out before.

Bhawana replied insensitively "Sorry, I am busy tomorrow I will catch up with you some other day" and abruptly cut the phone line. There was a moment of silence.

It was like someone had slammed the door hard on his face. Ashua did not know what to do next.

Should he call her again, this would make the situation even more awkward. So he decided not to call her. There was something else he had to do.

He decided to go to the Hariniwas colony where Bhawana worked and give her a piece of his mind about what he thought of Bhawana. He did not know if Bhawana was interested in him. She could have another man in her life. All these questions would be laid to rest only after meeting her. The next day, he dressed in his best outfit and went to Hariniwas Colony to meet Bhawana. As the colony was vast, finding the specific house where she worked proved to be a challenge. Undeterred, Ashua made his way to the main entrance gate of the colony and patiently waited for Bhawana to arrive.

Time passed by, and the wait became increasingly agonizing as there was no sign of Bhawana. Doubt started to creep into Ashua's mind, but his determination kept him going. Finally, after what felt like an eternity, Bhawana emerged from the colony gate, carrying a bag of fruits. Her presence illuminated the surroundings, and Ashua's heart skipped a beat.

Without hesitation, Ashua called out, "Bhawana, wait!"

Bhawana turned, surprised to hear her name. Her eyes met Ashua's, and a moment of recognition passed between them. The anticipation was palpable as they locked eyes, both aware of the unspoken emotions lingering in the air.

Bhawana was taken aback by Ashua's sudden appearance at her workplace, but there was a hint of curiosity in her eyes. She observed his earnestness and his genuine interest in getting to know her. Ashua quickly went towards Bhawana and without wasting any time asked her out.

He said, "Hi, You look really beautiful today. I have been waiting for you for a long time here at the gate but it's worth the effort. If you have time can I take you out for some coffee?"`

Bhawana smiled and nodded her head and said " OK."

As they walked towards the nearby café, a comfortable silence enveloped them. Ashua ordered coffee for himself while Bhawana quietly settled into her seat, a mix of excitement and nervousness in her demeanor.

Their conversation flowed effortlessly as Ashua shared his journey, his dreams, and the challenges he had faced along the way. Bhawana listened intently, hanging onto every word, finding herself drawn to his sincerity and passion.

Time seemed to slip away as they delved deeper into their stories. Laughter filled the air, and they discovered shared values and interests that only strengthened their connection. The hours melted away, and they were completely engrossed in each other's company.

As the evening wore on, Bhawana realized that it was growing late. Reluctantly, they knew it was time to part ways. They promised to meet again at the same café, their hearts already longing for the next encounter.

The following day arrived with an air of anticipation. Both Ashua and Bhawana had spent restless nights, their thoughts consumed by each other. The café became a sanctuary where they could freely express their emotions and share their dreams.

Their love was blossoming, and with each meeting, they grew more certain of their feelings. The future held endless possibilities, and they were eager to explore them together.

Every day, Bhawana and Ashua's bond grew stronger as they met at the café. Their conversations covered a wide range of topics, from everyday trivialities to their dreams and aspirations. Despite the simplicity of their discussions, they found joy in simply listening to each other's voices and being in each other's presence.

Ashua held Bhawana in high regard. He admired her unwavering determination and resilience, even in the face of adversity. Despite the loss of both her parents, she remained steadfast in taking care of her younger sister Riddhi and working hard to build a better life for them. He was inspired by her independence and her pursuit of education, as she attended night school to earn a degree in arts.

Bhawana's self-esteem and dignity were evident in the way she carried herself. She had enrolled in college to further her education, determined to achieve her dreams. She shared with Ashua her aspiration to become a schoolteacher, a profession that resonated with her heart. Although she acknowledged the current challenges she faced, she remained optimistic that things would improve.

In Ashua, Bhawana found everything she had ever desired in a partner. He was not only hardworking and dedicated, but he also possessed a great sense of humor that could brighten her darkest days. He cared deeply for her well-being, and his presence made her feel secure and loved.

Their connection was built on mutual admiration, respect, and shared dreams. Together, they supported each other's ambitions and found solace in their companionship. As their love blossomed, they knew that they had found something truly special in each other.

One day in the evening, Ashua noticed that Bhawana seemed distressed when they met at the café. Her eyes were filled with tears as she shared her frustrations about the constant complaints from the old couple she worked for. No matter how hard she tried, she could never seem to satisfy them. Bhawana expressed her desire to quit her job.

Ashua understood that he needed to provide a solution for Bhawana's problem. With a determined expression, he said to her, "Bhawana, we are in the midst of expanding our business. I am planning to buy a few more food trucks, and we will need dedicated individuals to run them. You can join me in running those food trucks."

Bhawana hesitated, uncertain about this new opportunity. As a woman, she had concerns about the challenges she might face. She voiced her doubts, saying, "I am unsure. I have never done something like this before, and it's going to be very difficult for me."

Ashua gently reassured her, "Bhawana, everyone starts somewhere. You have the strength and capability to overcome any obstacles. Believe in yourself and take that first small step. There is nothing a woman like you can't do when she sets her mind to it. Together, we can face any challenges that come our way, be a part of my journey."

His words resonated with Bhawana, and she started to see the possibilities. She felt a sense of empowerment and decided to take the leap. With Ashua's support and encouragement, she realized that she could overcome any gender stereotypes and pursue her dreams.

From that moment on, Ashua and Bhawana became partners in both their personal and professional lives.

With Ashua by her side, Bhawana knew she could achieve anything she set her mind to, and together they built a future filled with success and happiness.

Bhawana's decision to join Ashua in his journey filled him with joy and determination. He shared the news with Vikas, expressing his plans to expand their business by acquiring more food trucks and placing them in different parts of the city. This expansion would require them to hire more people, and Ashua happily revealed that Bhawana had become their first employee.

Vikas was thrilled by the prospect of expanding their business and the addition of Bhawana to their team. However, he was unaware of the challenges they would face on this new path. Ashua understood that building an empire would not be an easy task. It would require hard work, dedication, and overcoming various obstacles along the way.

Summary

Growth is the finest attribute of successful people.

Chapter 8

Growth is essential for any organization. They say change is the only constant. You have to grow and continuously improve yourself with each passing day. It's important to identify and eliminate your weaknesses while enhancing your strengths. Only then can a person truly achieve success.

Ashua was ready to take the risk of expanding his business. He knew there was no guarantee that his expansion plan would work, but he was willing to step out of his comfort zone. He understood that taking calculated risks is necessary to accomplish remarkable things in life. Ashua actually enjoyed engaging in activities that involved an element of risk. His past experience with making unconventional decisions had diminished his fear of failure.

With the earnings from his food truck over the years, Ashua decided it was time to invest in the expansion of his business. He planned to purchase two additional food trucks, each to be stationed at different locations in the city. The busiest streets of Charbattia would feature SUDHA food trucks. Ashua also wanted to enhance the branding of his trucks. He envisioned adorning them with beautiful neon lights that would proudly display the name "SUDHA FOOD TRUCK." His goal was for his food trucks to stand out among the rest.

If something had to be done, why not give it your best. The operation of these food trucks would be managed by Vikas, Bhawana, and himself. However, Ashua had another plan in mind—he wanted to hire additional staff to assist them. He required cooks to prepare the meals, waiters to take orders and serve customers, and dishwashers to handle the cleaning. But there was one crucial position he needed to fill—a Manager. This individual would oversee operations, guide the business in the right direction, and handle the expanding administrative tasks.

While Ashua and Vikas had been able to handle everything perfectly until now, it was time for a promotion within their organization. Ashua sought someone who could help them effectively manage the business. He wanted the individuals he hired to feel like they were part of an expanding family. Therefore, Ashua had to be extremely cautious during the hiring process, as one bad fish could have a negative impact on the entire team.

Ashua was on the lookout for the most talented individuals, but he understood that talent alone was not enough. Hard work was equally important, and he sought individuals who were dedicated and willing to put in the effort to ensure the success of their expanding venture.

Ashua believed that if something had to be done, it should be done with utmost dedication and effort. With that mindset, he envisioned running the food trucks alongside Vikas and Bhawana.

In his search for talent, Ashua prioritized qualities such as honesty and integrity. He believed that these traits were crucial for success in business. Talent alone would not suffice if a person lacked integrity and honesty. Ashua recognized that honest individuals were a rare breed, but their presence was essential for the smooth functioning of the business. Honesty required courage, especially in challenging situations, and Ashua valued those who displayed such bravery.

If you want to expand your business, building a strong and motivated team is crucial. A team that shares your vision and is driven to achieve success is the key to thriving in business. Like a jeweler searching for precious gems, Ashua was on the lookout for exceptional individuals. He searched for potential team members wherever he went, hoping to find the right people to join his expanding venture.

One sunny afternoon, as Ashua was walking down the street, he noticed a person who appeared lost in his thoughts. The man wore a blue shirt and black trousers and carried a folder in his hands. He seemed tired and worried, evident from the sweat on his forehead. Moved by his apparent struggles, Ashua stopped and approached the man, dropping a bundle of currency notes near him. Without drawing attention, Ashua slowly walked away, leaving the man to discover the unexpected gift.

The person noticed the money that Ashua had dropped and slowly picked it up. As he held the currency in his hands, his eyes lit up. He thought that the gods had suddenly been kind to him and that he should keep the money as a blessing. However, his inner voice reminded them, "You can't keep the money. It doesn't belong to you; it belongs to someone else."

Puzzled for a moment, he knew he had to make a decision. Since the money did not belong to him, he decided to do the right thing and return it to the true owner. But whose money could it be? They looked around and saw Ashua walking slowly in front of them.

Approaching Ashua calmly, he said, "Sir, can you check if you have dropped something?" He wanted to confirm if the money belonged to Ashua.

Ashua pretended to check his pockets and responded in a panicked tone, "Oh no, I think I have dropped my money."

The man looked satisfied because he had found the true owner of the money. He took out the money from his pocket and said, "Sir, I think this is yours," and handed it over to Ashua. As he started to walk away, Ashua stopped him and asked, "What's your name, young man?"

The person replied, "Nirmal."

Curious, Ashua asked, "What do you do?"

Nirmal replied, "I, sir, am looking for a job."

Ashua's excitement grew upon hearing this. He realized that he had potentially found the perfect manager to look after the operations of his expanding empire.

He said, "Young man, I just might have a job for you."

Nirmal was overjoyed at the prospect. It felt like his prayers had been answered. He had been searching for a job for a while, but without success. He had not expected this turn of events. God sends people to help people in various forms, and this time, it seemed that God had sent Ashua.

Ashua continued, "I am a businessman, and I am in the process of expanding my business. I require a manager who will be able to oversee operations and help me run the business."

He calmly took Nirmal to a coffee shop nearby and explained in detail his vision for expanding the business. He shared that he had a highly popular food joint on Melrose Street and wanted to extend its reach. His plan was to purchase more food trucks and place them in various locations across the city, essentially building an empire. He emphasized the need to recruit and train a team of individuals who could replicate the same level of culinary excellence and customer service that he and Vikas provided.

Ashua told Nirmal that each person was like a diamond, requiring shaping and polishing, and it would be Nirmal's responsibility to find and nurture these individuals. Nirmal quickly grasped the essence of Ashua's vision and decided to join his team. The salary offer exceeded Nirmal's expectations, sealing the deal.

With Nirmal on board, Ashua was relieved of the burden of recruiting and could focus on other aspects of the business. He understood the importance of trusting and hiring people who were better than him in specific areas.

Nirmal began the hiring process, seeking out individuals from various walks of life. His main criteria were loyalty and trustworthiness. After considerable effort, he assembled a team consisting of skilled cooks, attentive waiters, and diligent dishwashers, all handpicked by Nirmal.

Ashua took on the responsibility of training the newly formed team, imparting his culinary expertise. He emphasized the significance of precise ingredient proportions and highlighted that no task was less important than another. He instilled in them the value of teamwork, emphasizing that everyone's combined efforts were necessary to deliver the best possible experience to customers.

The training lasted for about a week, after which the new employees were assigned to different food trucks stationed across the city.

Ashua's "SUDHA" food trucks became an instant hit as soon as they hit the streets. Word had spread about their delicious food, and everyone wanted to try a bite. The trucks attracted a large customer base, and the cash counters manned by Vikas and Bhawana were bustling with activity.

Meanwhile, Nirmal took charge of the accounting and other administrative tasks, ensuring smooth operations. Ashua was actively involved in the background, managing tasks such as sourcing raw materials, maintaining inventory, and overseeing cash flow.

The influx of money multiplied several times over as the business flourished. Ashua and his team found themselves becoming wealthier with each passing day.

This level of success exceeded Ashua's expectations. They soon expanded their fleet, purchasing more trucks and hiring additional staff to keep up with the growing demand.

Despite the financial success, Ashua had a different dream in mind. Having experienced poverty and scarcity, he had a deep desire to give back to the society that had shaped him into who he was. He couldn't forget his village, Magaon, and the people who had supported him. Ashua wanted to do something special for them, but he knew he had to wait for the right moment to execute his plans.

After some time, Ashua became the owner of more than ten food trucks, and his reputation spread throughout Charbattia City, reaching even his brother Ramesh.

Meena, Ramesh's wife, frequently urged him to meet Ashua and reconcile, realizing that they had let a golden goose slip away. However, Ramesh was still plagued by embarrassment and hesitated to face Ashua after what he had done. The tides of time had changed, Ramesh and Meena started having arguments. Meena insisted that Ramesh should apologize to Ashua and seek his forgiveness.

Meanwhile, Ashua was fully occupied with expanding his business. His success surpassed all others in the city, and he generously sent large sums of money back to his father, Babuji. Occasionally, Babuji would visit Ashua in the city for a week or so, but he still preferred the peacefulness of village life.

Ashua had also provided employment opportunities to many people from his village, making him a well-known figure back home as well.

As the business continued to thrive, Ashua became a thorn in the side of his competitors. They resented him for capturing a significant portion of their market share, and now his presence was felt everywhere. One of these competitors was Dharam, who owned a food joint on Melrose Street. He had witnessed Ashua's meteoric rise with envy.

Dharam, a tall and lanky man with a prominent mustache, held the position of municipal member in the Melrose Street Association. As a shrewd politician, he always wore a smile on his face while secretly plotting to crush his rivals. He appeared friendly to Ashua, even feigning a close friendship.

One cold winter night, while everyone was asleep, Dharam devised a plan to sabotage Ashua. He quietly carried a can filled with kerosene to where Ashua had parked his food trucks. Swiftly and covertly, he poured the kerosene over the trucks.

Meanwhile, Nirmal, who was on his regular rounds, heard some suspicious noises coming from the direction of the food trucks. He paused, his senses alert, as he sensed something amiss. Before he could react, one of the food trucks burst into flames. He hurried to the scene, but it was too late to salvage the truck. There was no one nearby.

Nirmal quickly called the fire brigade, who arrived promptly. They managed to extinguish the fire before it could cause further damage.

Ashua arrived at the scene and caught a whiff of the strong smell of kerosene, he realized that his life's work was under sabotage. Someone was deliberately trying to harm his business and reputation. He knew that if he didn't take action, the situation could escalate further, potentially causing more damage.

Determined to protect his business, Ashua resolved to find the culprits and put an end to their malicious acts. He understood that he needed to be proactive and devise a plan to safeguard his trucks, employees, and the future of his expanding empire.

With a mix of frustration and determination, Ashua knew that time was of the essence. He needed to uncover the identity of those responsible and take necessary measures to prevent any future incidents. The battle had just begun, and Ashua was prepared to fight to protect all that he had built.

Summary

Each person is like a diamond, requiring shaping and polishing. None can change you unless you don't want to change.

Chapter 9

A s the investigation into the incident failed to yield any leads, Ashua realized that he had enemies lurking among the people he considered friends. It was a disheartening realization for him as he had always seen the good in others and trusted them. He couldn't fathom how someone could carry out such a treacherous act against him.

Although the damaged food truck had been repaired, the incident made Ashua acutely aware of the need to protect his business from future threats. He had worked hard to build his empire and wasn't willing to let anyone hinder his progress without a fight. He understood that he needed to gain power and influence to command respect and deter such malicious attempts. He wanted to get into the corridors of power.

Ashua recognized that power could bring about significant changes and enable him to positively impact the lives of millions. He desired to rise to positions of authority, understanding that people generally hesitated to mess with those in powerful positions. The pursuit of power became a form of resistance for Ashua, a means to safeguard his achievements and ensure that no one could easily undermine his efforts.

As for Dharam, he remained unsuspected by anyone. He held a respectable position in society and enjoyed the status of being the local president of the Melrose Market Association. Although this role was a small local designation, it held significant influence over the affairs of the market. The position was meant to be elected every two years through voting, allowing all market members to participate. However, Dharam had managed to win the election consecutively for six years and was now seeking to retain his post as the elections approached once again. His continuous victory reflected his hold over the market and the power he wielded within the association.

The elections were just a month away, and the anticipation among the people was palpable as they eagerly awaited the filing of nominations for the post of market president. One evening, Dharam discreetly entered Ashua's office while he was engrossed in paperwork with Nirmal. Ashua was taken aback by Dharam's unexpected presence, but greeted him with a hint of surprise.

With a disarming smile, Dharam extended his hand and exchanged pleasantries with Ashua. Ashua, curious about Dharam's visit, inquired about the purpose of his untimely arrival, suspecting that there must be something important to discuss.

Sporting the same grin, Dharam responded, "Indeed, I have something significant to discuss with you, Ashua. We have known each other for a while, and I have witnessed your remarkable growth and success in this market. Today, I come to you, my brother, with a request, and I am confident that you won't let me down."

Ashua's initial confusion lingered as he questioned Dharam, "What favor do you seek from me?"

With an air of confidence, Dharam revealed, "As you may be aware, the elections for the market president are imminent, and I am filing my nomination for the position. I merely need your vote and support."

Assuring Dharam, Ashua replied, "Don't worry, I am always there for you."

Dharam found solace in Ashua's reassurance, as he secured Ashua's vote in his favor. After expressing his gratitude, Dharam took his leave.

As soon as Dharam departed, Nirmal approached Ashua with an unsettling revelation. He confessed, "I don't trust that rascal. I wanted to tell you something a long time ago, but I wasn't certain. On the night our food truck caught fire, I believe I saw a man resembling Dharam fleeing the scene. The darkness prevented me from gathering concrete evidence against him."

Nirmal's disclosure struck a chord with Ashua, who peered into Nirmal's eyes and recognized the truth in his words. Disturbed by this revelation, Ashua pondered upon the fact that despite harboring no ill intentions towards anyone, there were individuals out there seeking to harm him simply because he had achieved success through hard work and vision. He wondered if his excellence and prosperity had become a liability, igniting jealousy among those who couldn't match his accomplishments. Ashua acknowledged that such adversities were often part and parcel of success, but he realized the need to change the perception of himself as an easy target.

Deep in thought, Ashua shared his next plan with Nirmal. He proclaimed, "Nirmal, I am going to run for the position of market president. If people want to play rough, I will also get rough."

Nirmal's face lit up with joy, delighted that his boss was ready to take on the challenge of running for market president.

News of Ashua's candidacy quickly spread throughout the city, carrying with it a sense of significance even though it was a local election. Dharam found himself rattled by the development, realizing that he now had a formidable competitor in Ashua, who enjoyed cordial relationships with the market members and had earned popularity within the market.

The following days witnessed a surge in efforts from Ashua, Vikas, Bhawana, Nirmal, and the rest of the team working tirelessly. They engaged in overtime, visiting market members and seeking their votes for Ashua. Each encounter reaffirmed their commitment to vote for Ashua, with many expressing their weariness of Dharam's reign and their desire for a change

Every evening, after a day's work, Ashua and his supporters embarked on a campaign trail, delivering speeches and seeking votes. Ashua made promises of transforming the market into a better place, free from problems, and attracting more visitors from the city. He assured people of a safer environment and encouraged them to approach him without hesitation if they encountered any issues. His speeches resonated deeply with the voters, drawing more and more people to his rallies. The voters began to connect with Ashua, seeing him as the embodiment of change.

A groundswell of support started to build in favor of Ashua. The concerns he raised struck a chord with everyone, as the issues were genuine and affected them directly. People yearned for a change and viewed Ashua as the new face of that change.

One day, as Ashua sat lost in thought, contemplating his next steps, he overheard a conversation among a group of individuals from the market. They were discussing the upcoming election.

One person asked, "Who do you think will win the election this year?"

Another replied, "I believe Ashua will win. What about you?"

At that moment, a voice chimed in, "But you know, Ashua is a wolf in sheep's clothing. I heard he ran away from his village and was caught stealing money from his brother's house. People are saying that he has spent time in jail for deceiving people and amassing his wealth. His own family has disowned him, so how can we trust him?"

Hearing these rumors being spread to tarnish his reputation hit Ashua hard. He listened silently, tears rolling down his cheeks. This was not what he had expected. It was a blow to his integrity and character. Nevertheless, he refrained from reacting outwardly. He knew that in love and war, nothing was fair, and this was indeed a battle.

The following day marked the nomination filing deadline, with the elections scheduled just two days later. Ashua, accompanied by Vikas and some of his supporters, went to the election commissioner's office to file his nomination. Ashua was in a somber state of mind, keeping to himself, but deep down, he retained faith in himself and his vision. Before entering the office, Ashua delivered a speech that would take everyone by surprise.

He began, "I want to express my gratitude to all of you for your unwavering support and well-wishes. It is because of your encouragement that I have come this far. However, I want to make an important announcement today. I have decided to withdraw from the race for the market association presidency."

The crowd was stunned, unable to comprehend Ashua's sudden decision. Ashua continued, "I have witnessed the power of rumors and lies that aim to tarnish my name. While it deeply pains me, I refuse to engage in a mudslinging contest. My purpose was to bring positive change to this market and uplift the lives of its people. I do not wish to participate in a process that deviates from that objective. I urge all of you to evaluate the candidates based on their merits, their vision for the market, and their commitment to serving you."

The election landscape had taken an unexpected turn, and the fate of the market association presidency was now uncertain.

The office was filled with astonishment and murmurs spread among the people. They felt foolish for having supported Ashua, believing they had been deceived.

Ashua proceeded to make an unexpected announcement, stating, "Since I am no longer in the running for the market association presidency, I nominate Vikas as my candidate for the position."

Silence fell upon the room. Vikas was caught off guard, completely unaware of Ashua's plan. He stood there, speechless, unsure of how to respond. In a loud voice, Ashua asked, "Are you with Vikas and me? Should Vikas be nominated as the candidate for the presidency?"

The office erupted with a resounding "YES" from everyone present.

Thus, Vikas became the candidate for the presidency, going up against Dharam. News quickly spread that Vikas was standing as Ashua's chosen candidate.

Two days later, the elections were held, and voters cast their votes in large numbers. It was a tense moment for Ashua and Vikas, who closely watched as each member of the market association cast their vote, trying to discern their allegiances.

Meanwhile, Dharam resorted to threats, pressuring people to vote for him and warning of consequences if they supported Ashua. In his frustration, he made declarations about destroying those who backed Ashua.

It became evident that the election had become a battle between good and ugly forces.

While Ashua had seemingly sacrificed his own candidacy, people believed that he had positioned Vikas as a figurehead, with Ashua wielding the true power behind the scenes. If Vikas won the election, he would be a mere puppet, with Ashua pulling the strings. It was a masterstroke by Ashua, strategically securing his influence.

Late at night, the election results were announced, revealing Vikas as the winner by a slim margin of ten votes. Despite the narrow victory, it was a triumph nonetheless.

The atmosphere turned jubilant, and everyone gathered at Ashua's apartment to celebrate. They congratulated Vikas on his historic win, as no one had defeated Dharam in the past six years. Vikas, overwhelmed with happiness, expressed his gratitude to Ashua for his victory. He never imagined he would become the president of the Melrose market association and credited Ashua for making it possible.

Summary

Power is attained by the powerful by right planning and right timing.

Chapter 10

The week following their victory was filled with festivities and immense joy. Congratulations poured in from all directions, recognizing their remarkable achievement of defeating Dharam, an opponent who had reigned unchallenged for the past six years. The spell that Dharam had cast over the market members had finally been broken, and his smooth talking had failed to sway them this time.

In a humorous twist of fate, even those market members who hadn't voted for Vikas joined in the congratulations, sporting wide smiles as they assured him of their support and belief in his victory. However, Vikas was well aware of their true allegiance to Dharam.

These were the cunning individuals who disguised themselves as allies but were ready to betray for their own petty gains. Vikas understood the importance of being cautious around such people, as they wouldn't hesitate to harm him. Nevertheless, in the realm of politics, one must maintain friendly relations with all and have no open enemies, so Vikas graciously thanked everyone, wearing a smile to hide his skepticism.

The following day, as a gesture of courtesy, Ashua and Vikas paid a visit to Dharam, who was still reeling from his defeat. Vikas reassured him that the election was just a part of the political process and winning or losing didn't mean they were enemies. He emphasized their shared goal of finding the best possible solutions to improve the Melrose Street market for the benefit of all businesses.

Inwardly, Dharam seethed with anger and resentment toward Ashua and Vikas, knowing that they had outmaneuvered him. He recognized the importance of keeping those in power close, adhering to the old adage of "keep your friends close, but keep your enemies even closer." He found himself in a helpless position against the duo who had skillfully cornered him.

Despite the veneer of cordiality, a sense of rivalry and tension lingered between Dharam and the newly triumphant Ashua and Vikas. The battle for dominance in the market was far from over, and each party knew they had to tread carefully and strategically to safeguard their interests and aspirations.

With Vikas's remarkable victory as the president of the Melrose Street Market, news of his achievement spread rapidly throughout the city. Everyone wanted to know more about this newcomer who had successfully defeated the influential Dharam. Conversations about Vikas and Ashua echoed from street corners to social gatherings, as their journey from humble beginnings to building a thriving chain of food trucks captivated the public's imagination. The duo's inspiring story of starting with nothing and now conducting business worth millions of rupees became a source of inspiration for many aspiring entrepreneurs. As word of their accomplishments circulated, Vikas and Ashua became household names, revered and admired in the city.

However, power and fame have a way of getting to one's head, easily altering egos. It is not easy to handle them. They are double-edged swords that can transform even the most virtuous individuals into beasts if not wielded wisely. Many have witnessed their lives crumble after working relentlessly hard and overcoming countless obstacles to attain power and fame, only to lose it quickly. Some succumb to the temptations of drugs and alcohol, while others, overwhelmed by the weight of their success, find themselves lost and eventually take their own lives. It is a treacherous realm to navigate.

Vikas, in the aftermath of his victory, found himself on cloud nine. Recognition poured in from all corners of society, attracting people from various walks of life who sought to meet him and extend their congratulations. Wealthy businessmen approached him, seeking favors and alliances. Vikas swiftly became a prominent figure in the city, his social circle expanding exponentially. He began to rub shoulders with the elite, receiving invitations to their extravagant parties, where copious amounts of food and drinks flowed. These gatherings boasted the finest delicacies accompanied by the best liquors the city had to offer. Initially, Vikas felt hesitant and out of place in these luxurious settings, overwhelmed by the glitter and glamour. However, he soon forged friendships with some of these individuals, and gradually, he became a regular presence at these high-profile events.

He had never experienced such lavishness before, and the temptations that accompanied it threatened to sway him from his grounded origins. The line between enjoying the fruits of his success and losing sight of his core values blurred. Vikas faced the delicate task of navigating this glamorous but treacherous terrain, all while ensuring that his rise to power remained rooted in integrity and a genuine desire to improve the Melrose Street Market.

Vivek had become one of the friends Vikas made along the way. Being the son of a wealthy businessman, Vivek lived a lavish lifestyle, flaunting flashy cars, fashionable attire, and being accompanied by beautiful women. However, Vivek had a destructive vice—he was an alcoholic who drank excessively. His drunkenness often led to quarrels and fights, but he was always bailed out by the deep pockets of his father.

As the saying goes, "A man is known by the company he keeps." Soon enough, Vikas started to undergo a troubling transformation, influenced by Vivek's negative traits. He became an hot-headed alcoholic, frequently venting his anger on his co-workers at the food truck for no apparent reason. The focus and vision that had once driven him had faded away.

Engulfed in his newfound company, Vikas began indulging heavily in alcohol. Nights would pass by in a blur as he stumbled into his apartment, losing track of time and direction. The partying and excessive drinking took him on a dangerous path, and despite Ashua's efforts to steer him away from this destructive behavior, Vikas turned a deaf ear. He neglected his work, showing no concern for his business. This behavior of Vikas as disturbing Ashua.

One unfortunate day, Bhawana approached Ashua with tears streaming down her face, leaving him traumatized by her distress. Concerned, Ashua inquired about the reason for her tears. Nirmal, who stood nearby, knew of what was about to unfold—Vikas was in serious trouble.

Bhawana, her voice trembling, revealed, "Vikas misbehaved with me today, Ashua. Ever since the win, he has changed. He asked me to meet his friend Vivek, but when I refused, he forcefully grabbed my hands, pushed me against the wall, and struck me. He has become abusive and violent. The victory has consumed his mind and soul. I can no longer work with him. You have to make a decision—it's either him or me."

With those words, Bhawana left, leaving Ashua seething with anger. His fury ignited, he wasted no time and immediately sought out Vikas. It was time to address the escalating situation, as things were spiraling out of control.

The worst decisions are often made in fits of anger, as anger clouds our ability to make rational choices. It blurs our logical thinking. However, on this day, that wisdom seemed elusive.

With a sense of urgency, Ashua rushed to the location where Vikas was sitting with Vivek, drowning himself in whiskey that had altered his behavior. The room was filled with suffocating cigarette smoke, and Ashua's immediate desire was to escape the atmosphere he had walked into. Amidst it all, a table at the center displayed a pile of cash, indicating a gambling session was in progress. Oblivious to Ashua's presence, Vikas and his friends were engrossed in their game.

In a burst of anger, Ashua bellowed, "Vikas!"

Vikas, bewildered upon seeing Ashua, struggled to maintain his balance under the influence of alcohol. He stumbled out of his chair and approached Ashua with a feeble voice, asking, "What happened to you, my brother? What brings you here?"

With firm resolve, Ashua responded, "I have been observing you closely, Vikas, and your recent behavior has become erratic and unacceptable. Today, you made a woman cry, someone who considers you like a brother. Can't you see where all this is leading you? It has become increasingly difficult to work with you. You no longer care about the business we worked so hard to establish. It pains me to say this, but our partnership has come to an end. You, my brother, are on your own."

Before Vikas could utter a word, Ashua slammed the door behind him, leaving Vikas standing there, left to grapple with the consequences of his actions.

It was indeed a sorrowful day for Ashua. The friendship that had endured countless trials and tribulations had suddenly and unexpectedly come to an end. People used to swear by their frindship, but now, it felt like the end of an era. "The inseparable had been separated, and it was a heartbreaking moment."

As Ashua arrived at his apartment, he was consumed by a mixture of anger and hatred towards Vikas. The intensity of his emotions made him want to throw everything out of the window. Vikas's thoughts lingered incessantly in his mind. Vikas was more than just a friend; he was family. They had accomplished so much together.

Feeling betrayed, Ashua experienced a deep emotional loss. He headed to the shower, where warm water cascaded over his body, and tears streamed down his face. The water from the shower seemed to wash away his tears, and though boys are often told not to cry and to remain strong, Ashua's tears silently subsided.

In his mind, Ashua held onto the belief that no one can take away his happiness unless he allows them to. These words echoed within him, and he refused to let Vikas steal his joy. Determined to move forward without him, Ashua contemplated how someone could be so foolish. Vikas had everything he had ever dreamed of, yet he had easily relinquished it all. The fascination of power had clouded Vikas's judgment, and there was no apology, no hint of remorse, nor any explanation for his despicable act of harming a woman. He remained motionless, frozen in time, leaving Ashua to grapple with the aftermath of their shattered friendship.

It was late in the evening, and Ashua, feeling weary, contemplated seeking some much-needed rest. However, just as he was about to settle down, the doorbell rang, jolting him from his thoughts. Intrigued yet cautious, Ashua made his way to the door, his heart pounding with anticipation. Opening the door, he was greeted by a sight that left him momentarily numb. Standing before him were some unexpected guests, triggering a flood of old memories that began to replay in his mind, evoking a mix of emotions within him.

Summary

It is easier to handle adversity than power. Power and fame is a two sided sword it can make or break you if not handled properly.

Chapter 11

shua found himself caught off guard by the unexpected arrival of these guests, especially at such a late hour. The memories associated with these people had haunted him in his sleep countless times, causing anxiety and despair to creep into his thoughts. As he stood there, contemplating whether to shut the door in their faces, his gaze lingered on Ramesh.

Yes, it was Ramesh, his brother, who had come accompanied by his wife Meena, cradling a small child in her arms. Ashua couldn't help but notice how frail and weak Ramesh appeared, struggling to maintain his balance on unsteady feet. A wave of sorrow washed over Ashua as he beheld his brother's pitiable condition, prompting him to invite them inside.

Curiosity and caution mingled in Ashua's voice as he asked Ramesh, "What brings you here brother?"

Ramesh, his face adorned with a broad smile, replied, "Brother, I have come to see you and congratulate you on your victory in the elections."

Ashua said softly "Thank you" and looked at the open door indicating them to leave. He had distanced himself from his brother, wanting nothing to do with him. Ramesh had been cast out of his sight and mind, as far as Ashua was concerned. The wounds inflicted by Ramesh and Meena upon Ashua still bore painful scars. Memories of being humiliated and thrown out of Ramesh's house were still fresh, making forgiveness an arduous task.

Meena, standing behind Ramesh, was in tears. Ramesh, his eyes welling up with moisture, pleaded, "Brother, please forgive me."

Ashua refused to entertain any more of his brother's pleas. Opening the door wide, he made it clear that there was no place for Ramesh in his life or in his heart. Ramesh turned to leave, accepting Ashua's unspoken message. However, Meena, determined to be heard, interjected, "Ashua, I am truly sorry."

Ashua paid her no attention, remaining resolute in his stance. Meena pressed on, desperation lacing her voice, "Please listen to me. Ramesh is very ill, unemployed, and we have nowhere to go. We have exhausted all our efforts to seek help, but no one is willing to lend a hand. This infant, our son and your nephew, please think of him".

Ashua felt a pang of sympathy as he glanced at the child nestled in Meena's arms. A mix of conflicting emotions washed over him—pain, anger, and a flicker of compassion. He closed the door partially, allowing a sliver of space for further conversation, his mind wrestling with the difficult decision that lay before him.

Ashua's voice trembled as he spoke, "The day you had me thrown out of your house spoke volumes about you, Meena. When I needed you the most, you were not there for me. You were my only support in this city, and you abandoned me without hesitation. I respected your decision then, and now I want you to leave and never show your faces to me again."

With those words, Ashua firmly shut the door, cutting off any further interaction with Meena and

Ramesh. Standing alone in the silence, he closed his eyes, engulfed by a wave of remorse and guilt. This wasn't the person he wanted to be, this cold-heartedness that prevented him from extending a helping hand to his own brother. They shared the same blood, the same lineage. Forgiving someone who had caused so much pain and haunted his memories was no easy task. There was an conflicting surge of emotions within him.

Contemplating his actions, Ashua moved to his balcony, seeking solace in the cool evening air. Doubt nagged at him—had he made the right decision by casting his brother away? As he gazed over the railing, his eyes caught sight of a familiar figure sitting on the pavement near his apartment. Though the area was dimly lit, there was a sense of recognition that stirred within him. Ashua hoped against hope that the person he saw wasn't who he thought it was.

Driven by curiosity and concern, Ashua descended to the pavement, approaching the old man who seemed oddly familiar. With each step, his heart raced, fearing the truth. Finally, he stood a few feet away from the person, and the realization struck him like a bolt of lightning—it was Babuji, with his weathered face and graying hair, his hands buried in despair as tears streamed down his cheeks. Ashua could hardly believe his eyes.

Not knowing what to do or say, Ashua cautiously approached Babuji and uttered, "Babuji."

Babuji, seemingly ignoring Ashua, began to walk away, his grief weighing heavily upon him.

Ashua's heart overflowed with emotion as he rushed towards Babuji, enveloping him in a tight embrace. Babuji stood there, seemingly detached from any expression of joy or grief, lost in his own thoughts. Ashua took hold of his father's hands and guided him back to his apartment.

Inside the apartment, Ashua prepared a cup of tea for Babuji, reminiscent of the old days when they would sit and talk for hours. Babuji, still silent, sipped the tea Ashua had made, allowing the warmth to comfort him.

Breaking the heavy silence, Ashua spoke softly, "Babuji, why didn't you tell me that you were coming?"

Babuji, a man who had witnessed his sons fight like dogs, remained silent, his thoughts locked away within.

Ashua made another attempt to coax words from his father, knowing the turmoil that must be raging

Ashish Sah

inside him. He continued, "Babuji, you're angry at me because I didn't help Ramesh."

The room seemed to hold its breath, waiting for Babuji's response. The weight of his silence was suffocating.

"You don't know what Ramesh did to me, Babuji," Ashua's voice trembled with the weight of his past. "He threw me out of his house, abandoning me when I had nowhere else to go. Only God knows how I made it this far without him."

Finally, Babuji broke his silence, his words carrying the wisdom of age. "Ashua, you have achieved so much. You have attained everything you ever dreamed of. But remember, true treasures lie in earning the love and respect of others. Material possessions may be with you today, but tomorrow they may fall into someone else's hands. What Ramesh did was wrong, but you are not an ordinary person. Forgive him. It will make you greater. From now on, strive to earn people's love and respect. Seek to earn people, not buy them."

Ashua listened intently to every word that Babuji spoke, understanding the profound lesson being imparted. Earning the respect of others, he realized, was an invaluable pursuit. It takes a lifetime to gain recognition and respect from people, but it had to begin within the confines of his own family.

While acknowledging that Ramesh's actions were unjust, Ashua recognized that he himself had not acted right in casting him away. Two wrongs do not make things right.

Realizing that everyone makes mistakes, Ashua saw the need to forgive Ramesh. Times had changed, and Ramesh was going through a difficult period. He had a child and nowhere to go. Babuji was hurt because Ashua had been unwilling to extend a helping hand to his own brother.

Taking a deep breath, Ashua made a firm decision. He whispered to himself, "Let bygones be bygones. I will invite Ramesh to stay with me, and I will offer him a job at one of our food trucks."

In that moment, a sense of peace settled over Ashua. He understood that forgiveness and compassion were the keys to healing the wounds of the past and building a stronger future for both himself and his family.

Ashua sensed that a burden had been lifted from his shoulder, which is the power of forgiveness.

It was late at night and Ashua escorted Babuji to his bed who was very tired. Ashua was sitting next to his bed and seeing him sleep peacefully was very satisfying.

It had been a very hectic day for Ashua. Today he had lost a friend but gained a family.

Soon Ashua shut his eyes and went to sleep only to be woken up by the ring of his phone. At first, Ashua decided to ignore the phone but it kept on ringing. He got up and took a look at the clock. Who would call him at 2 o'clock in the night? He was baffled. He picked my his phone.

On the other end of the line was Nirmal. He was in a state of panic and was murmuring things that Ashua could not comprehend. Ashua could not understand anything but he knew the situation was grave.

Ashua said slowly "Calm down Nirmal and tell me slowly what has happened?"

All Nirmal could say was "Hurry up! And Come to the Candy Hospital. "

Someone was not well and he had to go to the hospital. Ashua hurriedly changed his clothes and saw that Babuji was asleep. So he decided not to wake him and went to the hospital.

There in the hospital, he met Nirmal.

Ashua asked Nirmal what happened and why was he so upset.

Nirmal said, " Vikas is in critical condition."

This statement hit Ashua hard like a bolt of lighting. Although he despised Vikas and had a fight with him Ashua forgot all the differences and was ready for reconciliation. It was a day of forgiveness. A friend in need is a friend indeed.

Nirmal continued " Yesterday after you left the room Vikas had a heated argument with Vivek. Vivek said things about you and Bhawana that Vikas was not willing to take. The argument blew out of proposition and harsh words were exchanged between them. After which Vivek hit Vikas with a bottle on his head and he did not stop there. He beat him like a dog and his injuries have led to a lot of blood loss. He needs blood and we can't find any person with his blood group at this hour. Now it is unto you to save his life as you have the same blood group as him."

Nirmal paused for a moment as Ashua shook his head and said "Take me to him."

Ashua went to the ICU where Vikas lay unconscious. It was sad to see him laying there with his eyes closed. Ashua asked for the doctor and asked what needs to be done to save Vikas. The Doctor told him that his injuries were serious and that he needed blood which was of a rare group and they did not have it in their stock right now. Ashua offered his services as he had the same blood group. Ashua gave his blood to Vikas and stayed at the hospital the whole night next to Vikas unable to sleep.

The next day Vikas gained consciousness but he did not have the strength to speak. Doctors told Ashua that he was well but it would take time for him to recover.

After a few days, Vikas recovered.

Ashua met Bhawana and told him what had happened. How Vikas was caught in a fight with Vivek and asked her to come to the hospital to meet him. She was reluctant to come and meet him but Ashua told her to forgive him.

Ashua told her "Vikas is like a brother to you and in a family, people fight but it does not mean that they fight forever. There are differences in every family but differences must be resolved."

Bhawana agreed to meet Vikas and together with Ashua went to the hospital.

They reached the room where he was sleeping.

Ashua said softly "Vikas, look who has come to meet you."

Vikas slowly opened his eyes and saw Ashua and Bhawana standing next to his bed. His face lit up like a child who had found his lost toys. He smiled at them and held their hand and with all the strength he could muster said "Please forgive me Bhawana. I have hurt all the people that loved me but god has had his vengeance and it is painful. But today I promise you that we will be like a family just like the old days when we began this journey."

The Eyes of the trio were filled with tears and they hugged each other and held each other's hands firmly. Their friendship was the stuff of a legend.

Summary

Everybody has a family so we take it for granted. The bond within a family should never be broken.

Chapter 12

After Vikas was discharged from the hospital, Ashua took him back to his apartment and looked after for him. The whirlwind of events had caused Ashua to forget about his brother, Ramesh, who was living in a nearby slum. Babuji, staying with Ashua, grew increasingly anxious each day. Determined to address the situation, Ashua decided to visit Ramesh and Meena.

One day, Ashua set out to meet Ramesh. As he made his way, he caught sight of a beautiful villa—a white, spacious home with a delightful garden. The image stirred a vision of his own future, with children playing in the garden while their grandfather chased after them. The desire to own such a place consumed him. Midway to his destination, he contacted Nirmal, his trusted manager, and expressed his intention to purchase the villa. Nirmal, taken aback by the sudden urgency, questioned Ashua's motives but ultimately refrained from further inquiry.

Ashua arrived at the slum where Ramesh resided. The stench of the surroundings made him nauseous. Garbage cluttered the area, and people lived in cramped, tightly packed houses with a single shared toilet. The atmosphere was unsettling.

As Ashua walked along the narrow street leading to his brother's house, dizziness began to cloud his senses. The thought of turning back crossed his mind, but he persevered. Finally, he arrived at Ramesh's dwelling and gently knocked on the door.

From inside, he heard shuffling footsteps. The door creaked open, revealing Ramesh, appearing disheveled and weary. Ashua's heart sank at the sight of his brother's condition.

"Brother," Ramesh stammered, his voice filled with surprise and disbelief. "What brings you here?"

Attempting to maintain composure, Ashua replied, "I came to see you, Ramesh. I heard about your situation, and I couldn't stay away any longer."

Tears welled up in Ramesh's eyes as he stepped aside, allowing Ashua to enter the humble abode. The room was cramped, offering little space for a family to live in. Ashua's heart ached, realizing the stark contrast between his life of luxury and his brother's ongoing struggle.

They sat down, and Ramesh began to speak, his voice filled with regret and remorse. "I'm sorry, Ashua. I know I've done wrong to you. I was blinded by my own insecurities and made terrible choices. I never meant to hurt you."

Ashua looked at Ramesh, his gaze softened with compassion and understanding. He reached out, placing a hand on his brother's shoulder, feeling the weight of their shared history.

"Ramesh," Ashua began, his voice brimming with sincerity. "We have made mistakes, both you and I. But dwelling on the past won't help us move forward. We are a family, and family forgives each other. I am here to offer you a fresh start, a chance to rebuild what you once had."

Ramesh's eyes widened, his face a mix of disbelief and gratitude. "You... you would do that for me, Ashua?"

Ashua nodded, determination gleaming in his eyes. "Yes, Ramesh. It's time for us to leave the past behind and focus on the future. I have a place for you and Meena to stay—a comfortable home where you can raise your child. And I have a job for you as well, an opportunity to regain your independence and provide for your family."

Tears streamed down Ramesh's face as he embraced his brother tightly.

The following day, Ramesh gathered his meager belongings from the slum and moved into Ashua's apartment. Ashua allocated a room for his brother, ensuring that he had a comfortable space of his own. He believed in giving everyone a second chance and understood that nobody was perfect—mistakes were a part of being human.

Ashua instructed Nirmal to arrange training for Ramesh and assign him one of the food trucks to operate. Seeing his brother receive an opportunity for growth and independence brought Ashua immense joy and a sense of fulfillment. It was a remarkable achievement to be able to help and support his family in such a significant way.

Meanwhile, Ashua's dream of owning a house for his entire family was on the verge of becoming a reality. He initiated the process of purchasing the villa, engaging in negotiations and discussions. With each step, his anticipation grew. The prospect of having his future children reside in the villa, surrounded by their grandparents, uncles, and aunts, filled Ashua's heart with warmth. He cherished the idea of a joint family living together under one roof, creating a loving and supportive environment.

As the paperwork progressed, Ashua felt a sense of fulfillment, knowing that soon his dream would be realized. He eagerly looked forward to the day when his family would come together in their new home, where love and togetherness would permeate every corner. The house would truly become a home, a place where cherished memories would be made and treasured for generations to come.

Home, a place where love permeates every corner, and the bonds of care intertwine. In this haven, jealousy finds no refuge, and each individual stands ready to sacrifice for the greater good of the other.

For Ashua, life seemed to unfold in perfect harmony. His business thrived, with revenue pouring in from all the food trucks. The team operated as a tight-knit family, united in their endeavors. Profits soared, surpassing all expectations. It appeared that Ashua had discovered an unassailable path to success, where every endeavor yielded favorable results.

The harmony within Ashua's personal and professional life brought him profound contentment. He relished the fulfillment of building a prosperous business and witnessing his team flourish. The abundant prosperity he experienced seemed to confirm that he was treading the right path.

Yet, as the saying goes, success can be a double-edged sword. Amidst the elation of accomplishments, complacency stealthily crept in. Ashua became consumed by the momentum of his success, unintentionally overlooking the importance of vigilance and adaptability. Unbeknownst to him, the tides of the market were beginning to shift, and signs of change went unnoticed.

Slowly, the tides turned against him. Sales reached a plateau, and the once-soaring profits began to dwindle. It was a sobering wake-up call for Ashua, a reminder that even the most prosperous ventures required unwavering attention and foresight.

Soon, the Sudha Food Trucks stopped generating revenue, resulting in daily losses amounting to thousands of rupees. The balance sheet grew increasingly untidy, and Ashua's carefully built empire began to crumble. Ashua and Nirmal were at a loss, unable to comprehend the cause or find a solution. Worry and anxiety gripped them all.

After extensive analysis, they realized that it wasn't just their business taking a hit; the entire city was in a slump. A flu outbreak had engulfed the population, leading to a dire situation. Half of the city's residents fell ill, and tragically, some lost their lives. With no vaccine available, it was a nightmarish scenario. The government swiftly imposed a curfew, mandating citizens to stay in their homes. Public places were shut down, and only essential services operated under strict guidelines. The streets lay deserted, turning the once-bustling city into a ghost town.

Ashua's operations, like many other businesses, came to a grinding halt. The food trucks remained closed, with uncertainty shrouding their reopening.

Chaos and uncertainty prevailed. Ashua and his team were confined to their homes, unable to predict when life would return to normalcy amidst the relentless pandemic.

Despite the grim circumstances, Ashua made a courageous decision. While other businesses resorted to employee layoffs, he committed to paying his staff their full salaries. Recognizing the risk involved, he believed that by supporting his team during challenging times, their loyalty would be earned, a vital asset in sustaining a business.

As weeks passed, the virus loosened its grip, yet the situation remained dire. Most shops in the city remained shuttered, and only essential commodities were being delivered. Restless and determined, Ashua devised a plan, understanding that tough times called for resilience and innovation.

He gathered all his employees at his home, instilling a mix of anticipation and anxiety among them. Speculations arose, with fears of impending layoffs, a trend prevalent across the city. With families and financial burdens weighing heavily on their minds, they nervously awaited Ashua's arrival, anticipating sobering news.

When Ashua entered the room, he expressed gratitude for their presence and acknowledged the immense challenges they faced. He then unveiled his idea—a strategy not only to survive but to flourish in the face of adversity. They would transition their operations online, accepting orders over the phone and delivering meals directly to people's doorsteps. The city would be informed through newspaper advertisements, spreading their message of resilience. The team would consolidate meal preparation in one central location, while designated members would handle deliveries, recognizing the significance of food as an essential commodity.

A wave of excitement and unity swept through the room. The team rallied behind Ashua, embracing his vision wholeheartedly. The following day, the project was set into motion, with newspaper ads and a dedicated toll-free number for orders.

Ashua had meticulously organized every aspect of the operation. Team members efficiently took orders over the phone, skilled chefs prepared the meals, and dedicated delivery personnel swiftly transported the orders. Sudha Food Truck's presence was felt throughout the city as delivery personnel navigated the deserted streets, fulfilling orders. The business gradually regained momentum, and soon the volume of orders surpassed their expectations, necessitating the hiring of additional staff during the ongoing pandemic.

Ashua found himself generating more revenue than ever before, and a palpable sense of joy permeated the team. Against all odds, they had not only survived but thrived, emerging stronger in the face of adversity.

Summary
A man's true character is shown in times of difficulty.

Chapter 13

The havoc created by the coronavirus had left businesses reeling, with many on the verge of closure. It was a city-wide catastrophe, and people everywhere felt the impact of the virus. Restaurants, in particular, were among the hardest-hit establishments. However, Ashua stood strong amidst the chaos, his coffers filled with money.

Unlike others, Ashua was not one to give up easily. A man who refuses to surrender cannot be defeated. Such resilience is a defining characteristic of successful individuals. With businesses crumbling around him, Ashua's enterprise remained an exception. Money was flowing in rapidly, and he began contemplating what to do next. However, he kept these thoughts to himself, patiently waiting for the right opportunity to arise.

Gradually, the grip of the virus began to loosen on the city. Slowly but surely, life started returning to normalcy. The discovery of a vaccine brought hope, and people eagerly lined up for their doses. Shops reopened, and the city started to regain its pre-pandemic vigor. Amidst the carnage that had befallen many businesses, Ashua saw an opportunity to make the best of the situation, as the market was at an all-time low. The time had come to take the next step.

Ashua set his sights on acquiring a restaurant, as he had already established himself as the king of food trucks. One day, Nirmal approached Ashua with news that a restaurant, which he might find intriguing, was up for sale. Curiosity piqued, Ashua casually inquired, "Which restaurant?"

Nirmal replied, "DARBAR."

Ashua's eyes lit up with excitement. It was the place he had always yearned for deep in his heart. DARBAR, where he had worked and honed his culinary skills, held a special place in his memories. He owed so much to that place. Unable to contain his enthusiasm, he exclaimed to Nirmal, "Let's go for it!"

After a few days, a meeting was arranged between the owners of DARBAR and Ashua. Numerous rounds of intense negotiations took place, but eventually, the deal was sealed, and Ashua became the proud owner of DARBAR—the very place where it had all begun.

It was decided that DARBAR would undergo a transformation, and the restaurant would be relaunched with a new name. This time, it would be called SUDHA, signifying purity. All necessary preparations were made to beautify the place. Flowers were meticulously arranged, old furniture was replaced with new pieces, and the interior underwent a complete makeover. Everything old was discarded, marking the beginning of a new chapter.

To celebrate the opening of the restaurant, Ashua invited everyone near and dear to him. As the guests assembled in the hall, Ashua observed them closely, scanning the room for one special guest. Suddenly, his heart raced when he spotted her among the crowd.

Stepping into the hall, a flood of memories overwhelmed Ashua. It was the same hall where he once served meals as a waiter, reminiscing about the excitement he felt whenever a generous customer left a generous tip. The place still exuded the same vibe, despite some changes in staff. Mr. Lalit, who had mentored Ashua, still ran the kitchen. One thing caught Ashua's attention—the dishwashing area remained untouched. That corner symbolized the start of his journey into the city, transforming him from a dishwasher to a restaurant owner. It was not a miracle but the result of sheer hard work, determination, and the will to overcome obstacles.

As people saw Ashua enter the hall, a hush fell over the room. Then, thunderous applause erupted, lasting for several minutes. Everyone knew that Ashua had once worked in the very restaurant he had now acquired, and they recognized the significance of his achievement.

Filled with pride, Ashua called upon all the founding members of his team to join him on the podium. He urged the guests to applaud his team, recognizing their contributions. Vikas, Nirmal, and Bhawana—all took their place on the podium, basking in a sense of pride and accomplishment. In that moment, they knew they had made it.

Taking control of the proceedings, Ashua asked Bhawana, looking radiant in her blue dress, to step closer. With all eyes on them, he asked the question

Bhawana had long been waiting for: "Will you marry me?"

The unprecedented chain of events brought smiles to everyone's faces. The crowd roared, chanting, "Say yes!" Blushing, Bhawana shyly replied, "Yes."

It was Ashua's day of triumph. Feasting and dancing filled the air as everyone celebrated joyously. The people Ashua had invited were those who loved and cherished him, wishing only the best for him. They didn't want this moment to pass.

The following day, Ashua decided to visit his village, Magaon. As a small village, news of Ashua's accomplishments had spread far and wide, making him an inspiration to many. Accompanied by Ramesh, Meena, Babuji, and Bhawana, he set off for his hometown. The villagers gave him a hero's welcome, showering him with flowers as a sign of respect. Not much had changed in the village since his departure. Radha continued to work in the fields with other village women, Mukesh the milkman still tended to his cows, and the village roads remained as poorly maintained as ever.

Ashua headed to his house, which had undergone significant expansion, now a spacious structure unlike any other in the village. However, despite the modern amenities, it lacked the warmth of the past. Ashua longed for the goats he used to graze and the cozy rooms where he and Babuji would sip tea and gossip. His connection to the house seemed lost. But as he opened a window and looked outside, he saw the mountains where he used to take his goats to graze. He recalled the temple where he had encountered the monk.

Without hesitation, he embarked on the familiar path leading to the mountaintop. As time passed, he found himself growing weary, his breath becoming labored. Eventually, he had to rest on a rock along the way. This was the same path Ashua used to climb effortlessly. The city had taken a toll on his stamina, but his determination to reach the temple remained unwavering. He wondered if the monk would be there, waiting for him, hopeful for another glimpse of the holy one.

Finally reaching the mountaintop, he washed his face with the crystal-clear water flowing from a stream. He then made his way to the temple. As he caught sight of the sacred place, his heart filled with joy. Moving closer, he noticed that it appeared exactly as it had before, except that the encroaching undergrowth had claimed half of the temple. The moss had painted the structure green.

Ashua searched the vicinity, hoping to find someone present, but it was to no avail. No one had visited the temple in a long time. He scoured the area, yet no one except the deafening silence greeted him.

Ultimately, Ashua sat before the temple, closed his eyes, and offered a prayer of gratitude to the holy one for the guidance and blessings he had received. His heart remained as pure as the air surrounding him.

After a moment, a voice reached his ears. "Ashua, you have accomplished what you set out to achieve. People now respect and love you not just because of your wealth, but because of your character. Your dreams have become a reality, and I am proud of you. Now, with the recognition and influence you have gained, it is your responsibility to use your power to make a positive change in society. Help those you encounter and work to create a better world, for you are the chosen one."

Ashua slowly opened his eyes, half-expecting to see his mentor standing before him. However, no one was there. Perhaps the monk had only existed in his imagination, yet it had guided him to the mountaintop. Ashuastood up and slowly went behind the temple and the footprints of the monks were vaguely visible. Ashua touched the footprints with boths his hands to seek his blessing. His dream to build a school and a hospital in the name of his late mother resonated in his heart.

After wandering in the woods for sometime Ashua sat at the ridge near the temple and as he set his eyes on the setting sun he felt that he had a deep connection with the universe. He felt like he and the universe were one and the universe had always been listening to him and he had been guided by the universe to reach so far.

And as a gentle breeze caressed his face, Ashua closed his eyes once more, feeling the chill in the air. The wind's touch felt like a blessing, reminding him that there was still so much to accomplish in life and encouraging him to never give up on his aspirations.

Ashish Sah

Milton Keynes UK
Ingram Content Group UK Ltd.
UKHW021138010424
440413UK00007B/108